T0103447

Churning Out Success Formulae

Churning Out Success Formulae

"The ancient technique of
learning and applying science
of becoming successful"

Ankit Shende

PARTRIDGE
A Penguin Random House Company

To order additional copies of this book, contact
Partridge India
000 800 10062 62
orders.india@partridgepublishing.com

www.partridgepublishing.com/india

Contents

This <u>Book Dedicated to my Father</u> who not only supported me in every walk of Life but also inspired me, motivated me and given me freedom to do any work or decision I have ever made. I'm really thankful and appreciative for your love, efforts and understanding towards me.

"<u>My Father is my Hero and role model</u>"

Okay okay I know you are waiting to hear your name "<u>Maggi</u>", I present you this <u>book as a gift "Maggi" with all my heart</u>. I found only key when I'm far away from you to keep your troubles at bay throughout your life even when you are alone on the life path. This gift will lift your spirits in tough times and give you the strength to do whatever you set out there to attain true happiness in life. I'm really thankful and appreciative for all your efforts of pouring happiness into my life.

"<u>I always wanted to do something great and good for you and dad, so that you should be proud of me</u>, these are the reason why I kept on holding so long. I have no expectation from you or anybody and yes off course I love you a lot."

Really appreciative of sharing your life moments with me which poured happiness and Special Thanks for your encouragement like Amit pal singh Bagga, Rishu katoch, Mukesh and Vandana Malakar (close buddies who were there in thick and thins of life), Joel Ashish Sir, Akansha Ingle, Suvidha kamble and Arjita Singh my cousin, Varun tyagi (chuddi buddi bittan I know you are always there), Shoeb Ahmed (shaju supporting for meditation), Praveen (jumbo), Pravesh tiwari sir, Ashish ingle (ingad), and Rakesh Zade Sir.

I'm really thankful to all my friends being there and really appreciate for sharing your time which brings splash of happiness in my journey of life D Bhavana (one of my best friends), Prajkta my sister, Manisha Agarwal, Sonu Kaul, Vishal Kataria, Ashwin Sahare, Shivaji Naikude, RKP mama ji (Rajesh kumar pandey great encourager), Gaurav Pandey(Goldy), Rupesh & Nitesh Shende, Vivek sharma, Maninder (pajji), D Ramya, Ashna ramju, Isha, Dr. Archana, Sid, Harsh Goyal, Shilanand Gajbhiye, Garima (gabbu don), Sonam and Abhishek Jaiswal, Vaibhav Henry, Vivek sethi sir, Ashish warkar, Gulab singh sir, Kushal dhole, Atish Dhatrak, Vinod Modiwale, Pradeep singh, Mayank Nayak, Atul Tripathi, Vinay bharti (pakdu), Mayur kashyap (jabra), Vipin Sarate, Jitendra singh, Puneet saxena (kater) and Mohit Gupta (baba), S. Anant, Saurabh Panda, Kaushal kishore (K.K Shooter) and Rachana Sharma, Neeraj (Lavvi), Ashok Pali (paliye), Sapan Gujarati (Sapola), Nasim Khan (Chacha), Ankur malik (Sloth), Beth (online guitar teacher), Poonam, Swati and Rashmi mam, Mithila Kukdolkar, Soham Dasgupta, Digvijay Deshmukh, M.M Shah (janu), Prajwal, Chandan Deshpandey, Piyush Deshlehra (pichus), Shantanu Vyas, Priyanka kukereja, Atul and Vipul singh, Anshul, Dau and Patel, Shweta thadani, Priyaj Vindekar, Ashish vishwakarma, Jagdish Makana (Jaggu), Harry Iyer, Tamojit sengupta (Tammo), Shakti Chauhan, Ankit Bharadiya, Sumit & Shweta Gharu, Vinay Jain(Jaini), Nilesh Naik, Pranav shirode, Nadeem Nizami, Sagar Chandra, Suhail (Sukel) Rizvi, Shivan Sathpathy, Shivendra, Risha mam, Sameer dehadrai sir, my both mom, Amit raj, Vishal lala sir (lale di jaan), Sandeep Rawat Sir (cindy crowft), Jaspal Singh Birdi Sir, Vikas Rohit Sir, Amit Kumar Sharma Sir, Manish Sir, Veena rajawani Mam, Manju mathur mam, Madhuri Chandrakar mam, Ratna Tondon mam, Tessi mam, Rekha Nikhare (Bua), Padmini Meshram (Bua), Nishant & Rashika Nikhare and many more.

Surprisingly I had largest family in this world with you all as member of it and no doubt I'm the most beloved one.

Unconditional love of Abhishek my brother towards me, it's a gratitude and blessing for you from my side.

I love you all, that's the way I'm. It is hard to improve perfectionist like me only smiles and flourish this happiness to others no claps please.

With lots of love

Ankit Shende

Success Cycle

Like the number Lock can be unlocked with correct combination of key numbers in similar fashion you can tap correct combination of quality present within you to unleash the unlimited power which will bring one hundred percent success and fill your life with colours of purpose, happiness and contentment.

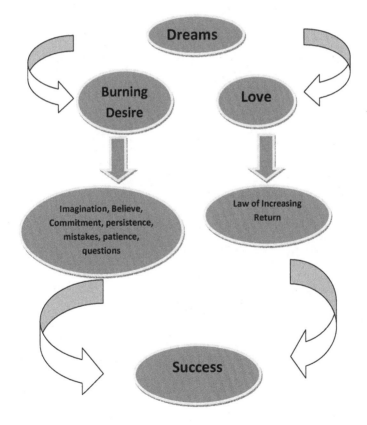

The ancient technique of learning and applying science of becoming successful

This book is specially designed using ancient technique of learning which was used by one of our sage in India to teach his students called "Panchtantra" this is an art who's purpose was to make them learn with the help of stories by making it more interesting, later his students were wisest men in the town.

The very first thing you have to notice about the book is that all this qualities were also discussed in Geeta and I consider lord Krishna as god of success because I found him one of the successful super human of his time. His teachings were purely on the basis of successful living because he always succeeded in keeping trouble at bay while others have invited as a part of their being. Although I had gone through Bible and I considered it most positive inspirational book man can read and apply its principle in life. I had also read various literatures about Buddha and his teachings also which depicts mostly living with peace of mind. I want to make note to all people that I'm not against any religion or caste just I want to convey humanity is the uppermost religion for all of us and we should take good part of every holy book and their preachers teaching whether it's Jesus Christ teachings or Prophet Teachings or Guru Nanak Teachings or Buddha teachings because I personally love all of the saint who tried to impart the teachings of humanity, healthy and prosper living but we humans distorted their words and teachings for our own benefits.

Well to all readers I had also written this book for those who want to leave the legacy behind, who are in search of success. This book will not only uplift your spirit but will make you understand because with understanding only you can truly be guided for success.

Chapter – One

"Life is a projection of what we dream at some point of Time – Ankit Shende"

Everyone of us know or look around us have some form of beginning, the origin point from where it started his journey like river it starts somewhere from the mountains and end up in ocean in similar way every success starts from the seed of dreams. Our life is a projection of what we dream at some point of Time. It starts with dreams and goes on with it till the end. Have you ever seen new born baby, you will observe he sleeps most of the time but when you look at him closely you will find various expression on his face while sleeping and what we say "Baby is dreaming". Everyone of us has dreams, as child we have dream of becoming big boy, when we had walk down the stores as a child with our parents we looked at bicycle then we had dreamed of having one, when we watched other kids playing play-station we had dreamed of having one and when we grew up we start dreaming of becoming lawyer, doctor, engineer, best sportsman, businessman etc, in every walk of life we have dreams. Dreams are the wheel on which earthen pot of life is made by our own capabilities. Every real life success story starts with dreams, so never stop dreaming. Many people don't think worthy to dream big but if you want to produce astonishing results out of life you have to dream big because every dream is possible no matter what may be your circumstances to summon up the thought I will illustrate this with a story around the real life of a common man.

The young man who was the son of a mason who would go from market to market sell vegetables with mother and in the evening would sell balloon's to support his family of four sisters, mother, father and grandmother. As a result, the boy's high school career was interrupted and he scored less grades. When he was in senior school at annual function conducted by school, he participated in an extempore competition, it's a competition in which person is given a topic and you have to think for two minutes and speak after that on stage, the young boy got the topic "Dreams".

After two minutes of hard thinking he came up with his dream about what he want to become in life and what he want to do when he will be grown up. He started his speech with goal of becoming Doctor. He spoke about his dream in great detail and he with his words and body language made audience realize of Nursing home, showing the location of rooms, operation theatre, medical store and his house.

He put a great deal of his heart into his speech and as everybody busted into laughter. One of the judges was his teacher told him to meet after competition.

The Boy with dream went to see the teacher after competition and asked why students laughed and he didn't even have appreciation for his speech?

The Teacher said "This is an unrealistic dream for a boy like you. You have no money and you belong to poor family. You have many responsibilities of family. You have no resources to go for medical studies and owning a nursing home and house requires lot of money. To Support your college education you have to spend lot of money on books, college fees, hostel fees and later you have to pay large amount to buy a land and towards construction. There's no way you could ever do it."

Then teacher added think with more realistic goal which can be accomplished because this goal is impossible for you and you have to drop this dream as you are always slipping on grades in studies.

The boy went home and thought about it long and hard. He told his father whole incident and asked what should he do? His Father said "Look son, you have to make up your mind on this because your teacher is right and I thought of making you advocate which is great profession and affordable to me." But boy was determined to become Doctor and said to father "I have strong desire to be Doctor and I will not change my decision." This annoyed father he threw him with all force on the floor and boy hand got fractured because of it, Than there was meeting called by gathering whole neighbours by his father so that by pressurizing he would change his decision but when they all look his determination and decided that if he failed or dropped even once he will have to follow his father's will. Finally, three days later the boy turned to teacher with no changes in his decision and dream.

He stated "I have decided not to quit on my dream."

After many years at inauguration ceremony of nursing home he invited his teacher and all people who were there at that time and made recalled everybody the old story. The best part of story is that his father said "Look son, at that time I had made up my mind that it cannot be achieved and compromised with our circumstance that it will never change and I was something of a dream stealer of my every children, all five of you but fortunately you were determined enough to accomplish your dreams.

This is a Real Story of Dr. Sukhdeo Shende born on 19th september 1954 who despite of many challenges accomplished his dreams, he also faced challenge of being paralysed for complete one year due to brain tumour, gone bankrupt due to illness and responsibilities of his family.

So don't let anyone steal your dreams because it always seems impossible until it is done.

Everyone of us see dreams now the question comes how to identify that dream which you really want to accomplish, which will give life it's meaning and which will give life its purpose? The answer to this question is present within everyone of us, it is the vision of future which will do often come to you somewhere in the middle of some work or while sleeping, it will be constantly whispering into your ear ringing like alarm clock, it will infuse strong urge in your heart to accomplish it. In silence when you are alone, you will observe glimpses of it will give new hope, butterflies in your belly and your whole inner body react to it. Most of people give up on their dreams never realizing that true happiness can never be achieved until they accomplish their dreams. The fact says it can't be done today and people find reasons, excuses and then they claim they don't want it anyway. This very nature of human can be understood by a fable. Long ago in the dark, dense and deep forest there lived a fox. One day fox was wandering sawed a mango tree. Fox wanted to eat some delicious mangoes because mangoes were hanging from a branch just enough high above the ground that fox had to keep jumping and jumping in order to reach them.

After lots of tries and a long while fox gave up on his dreams by claiming that he didn't want mangoes anyways because they are sour But it's not true. People also gave up like the fox in the story and then they claim that they never wanted it or they didn't able to do it because of him, her or anybody and find excuses to justify their act to quit.

But the true fact is "Achievers are great Dreamers". Once a press reporter interviewing successful businessman said "It's a miracle that long back you were homeless and now you turned out to be riches of the town." The young businessman smiled and said "Miracles start to happen when you give as much energy to your dreams as you do to your fears." The reporter little amazed then asked "What Does Dreams means to you???" The businessman said "It means glimpses for the future that will capture your entire heart and at the deepest level of your spirit and soul."

Then reporter said "not every dream come true you got to be lucky."

To his amuse businessman again stated "All dreams can come true, small dreams take less time while big ones require a lot more." Then Businessman started narrating story to elaborate his vision, he said "There were two seeds lying side by side on the fertile soil, the first seed said "I wanted to grow up, lay my roots deep down inside and sprout from the ground. I have a dream to blossom in delicate buds and proclaim the coming of spring. I want to feel the warm rays of sun and the dew drops on my petals." This seed grew up and become a beautiful flower.

The second seed said "I'm afraid, if I will put down my roots into the ground. I don't know what they will face there. If I will grow tender stems, they will be damaged by winds, season and surrounding temperature and if there will be flowers, they may be disrupted. So I had rather wait for safe time."

The second seed was waiting while a bird came and pecked it.

So it is important that you have dream, nurture it, protect it and with time be ready to make that dream come to reality.

Some people go through life being a mediocre, they earn a living, raise a family and then they die. Never try to stretch them or make anyway waves, never try to know what's possible for them. They become satisfied like the frog living in the well. This parable will truly depicts our undermine nature responsible for our mediocrity.

There was a frog, which lived in the dark, deep well. The well was very old filled with shallow water at the bottom. The wall's all covered with wet moss. When frog was thirsty and hungry, he would drink the well water, catch some insects and ate them. When he was tired he would lay on a little rock at the bottom of the well and looked up the sky above him. He saw passing clouds and nights full of stars. He was satisfied and happy.

The little frog was living at the bottom of this old well since he was born. He was never been to the outside world. Whenever birds flew by and stopped at the edge of the well, the little frog looked up and asked them to come down and play with him. He would insist them "it is pleasant down here, cool water to drink and plenty of insects to eat. At the day time, sometimes I can see the clouds passing and in the night I can watch the twinkling stars and sometimes I can see the beautiful moon."

Sometimes the birds would tell the frog "You know, outside world is much bigger and nicer place to live. It is more beautiful than your little well at the bottom". But frog would not believe them and tell them "Don't lie to me, I don't believe there is any place that could be beautiful than here."

Due to his stubborn behaviour, gradually all birds began to disliked him and later stopped talking to him. The frog never figured out or able to understand why nobody would like to come down to his place.

Day's passed on and after long one day a sparrow came to the edge of well. The frog became excited, greeted the sparrow and eagerly invited by enthusiastically explaining the same old description of the well. The sparrow didn't say a word and flew away. The next day the sparrow came again and the same thing happened again. It went on for a week like this and finally after a week sparrow said "Little frog may I show you the outside world?" But the frog refused the offer and sparrow flewed away.

The next morning she came again and frog started insisting again to come down to his home, looking his stubbornness sparrow decided and flew to the bottom of the well picked up the frog and flew out of the well.

Frog in amazement once it was out of well said "How it is the world outside is so big?"

Frog eyes blinked and he could barely able to open his eyes in the bright sunshine due to his prolonged living in the bottom of dark well.

Finally when he became comfortable with bright light, he saw so many things around him. He asked sparrow "what is that big and low strange green things in between of our way. Sparrow happily replied "These are mountains and valleys. The next view made frog little more surprised.

He asked again "what is that long, shiny thing down below?"

Sparrow said "It is a river" and after that she indicated down towards north east and said "Look over there that huge blue thing that is a sea."

Frog started thinking river and sea hold billion times more water than his well. He began to realize how tiny was his world down there in the well. He said to sparrow "Let's go down." The sparrow put the frog down on the ground and flew away.

Frog jumped into the grass, saw many beautiful flowers of different colours smelled there nice scents, he further went to forest sawed many tress and fruits on the ground tasted them, listened to the birds singing and monkeys swinging from branch to branch.

He jumped towards the pond wondering and looking at the beautiful lotus dancing and floating in the water and there were many fishes also in the water. The tears run down his eyes of joy and happiness seeing the outside world so big, beautiful and wonderful. Finally he jumped into the pond welcoming his new life.

People become satisfied and comfortable with their life like the little frog. They stop pushing themselves and then they close the curtain of the screen of their dreams. One should know the truth until or unless if you don't pursue your dreams, you cannot attain true happiness and life would be meaningless if you can't be happy.

Allow your dreams to guide your life, it will give your life sense of purpose to live with its true Colours and remember we are the only who can kill our dream; it is within us the power to live or kill our dream. So don't kill your dream rather live your dreams.

You have to understand that dreams are the roots to recognizing and embracing the potential for greatness within you.

Hold on to your dream, things will not work for time being or it will not happen as quickly as you want it to be or the way you want it to happen but if you have vision or deep desire for that dream it will happen in some other way or in much bigger sense you could ever imagine. Let me share with you a textbook story which had inspired me to never stop dreaming, Long ago three giant trees dwell along the border of the deep forest over the hill. They were friends for years facing many seasons together in joy and sorrow. One day they were sharing their hopes and dreams with each other. The first tree said "I have a dream that one day I will be transformed into an elegant treasure chest with decorative intricate carving which could be filled with gold, silver, precious gems and jewellery". Then the second tree said "My dream is to become a mighty ship carrying kings and queens across the water and sailing to the corners of the world making everyone feel safe in me because of the strength of my hull". Finally the third tree said "Although we are tallest and straightest tree in the forest still my dream is to become more taller, magnificent and giant tree to be remembered through the history because people can see at this hill top and look up to me thinking of how close I'm to the heavens and god".

Few years passed by with holding on to their dreams and praying that it would come to reality, one day a group of woodsmen came upon the trees. One of the woodsmen looked upon the first tree and said "This looks like a strong tree which can be used by carpenter; I think I would be able to sell the woods of tree to carpenter for few bugs". He began cutting it down. The tree became happy hoping his dream will be finally fulfilled when he would be taken to the carpenter, where carpenter would turn him into a treasure chest. The next woodman standing in front of second tree said "This tree looks quite strong; I should be able to sell it to the shipyard". The second tree became happy because he knew his journey of becoming mighty ship had started. Finally one of the woodsman arrived to the third tree, upon this the tree became frightened because once he was cut down his dream will be crushed and will never come to reality. Woodsman said "I don't have any specific needs, so I will take this one" and he began to cut the tree.

When the woodsman sold the first tree to the carpenter. Carpenter took the woods and made it into a animals feed box. He was then placed in a barn and filled with hay and fodder for the animals. This was not at all what he had been dreaming and praying for. The second tree was brought to the shipyard and being transformed into a small fishing boat eroding his dream of becoming a mighty ship and carrying kings along the corners of the world. The third tree was cut down into large pieces and woodsman left it into his fields. The years went on passing and with sand of times trees starting to forget their dreams.

Suddenly one day, a man and woman came to the barn to stay as woman was having pregnancy pain. She gave birth to beautiful baby that was placed on the hay in the feed box made from the first tree. The man wished that he could had made a crib for the baby but thought this manger will serve the purpose. The tree could feel the importance of the event took place and knew that his dream is fulfilled in much greater sense beyond his expectation by holding the greatest treasure of all time. Few years later, group of men got in the fishing boat made from second tree into the water. One of the gentlemen felt tired and went to sleep. While they were sailing on the water suddenly a great storm arouse and the tree doubted his ability to withstand the storm and keep safe the men he was carrying.

One of the men went to wake the sleeping man and as he stood and said "Peace" the storm stopped. By the time event happened, the tree came to knew that he was carrying the kings of kings in his boat. Finally one day someone came and got the woods of third tree. It was carried through the street as the people mocked the man who was carrying it. They came to the top of the hill where this man was nailed to the tree and raised in the air to die and by the Sunday, tree came to realization that he was strong enough to stand at the top of the hill as much close to god as possible with god's own son Jesus crucified on it.

With this thought I insist you to open your heart, mind, body and soul to the wonderful power of your dream. Give your creative imagination the courage and freedom to dream of what life could be one day and begin the process of dreaming.

"To make your dream come true you not only have to feel it rather breathe it, live it every single moment until it is not achieved. – Ankit Shende"

Self Help Assignment:-

- Think & Fill down all your potential dreams which you want to achieve dividing them into three major categories

  Personal:-

  Financial:-

  Social:-

Fun Activity to be practised:-

1. Take a Sheet write down the dreams you have charted out in self help assignment and paste it in front of bed.

    Daily before you go to sleep or wake up in morning you must see it and think about your dreams for five minutes.

2. Make a Vision Board where you can paste all the pictures of the things you want to have in your life put it near to mirror and review it while you are in front of mirror once in a day.

Chapter – Two

"Our Desires sets up the stage for our visions – Ankit Shende"

Albert Einstein given us words of wisdom "Necessity is the mother of all inventions" which are true to its verdict. In similar fashion you have to test your dreams in the fire of desires. All human activity is prompted by desire, to keep your go getter attitude towards your dream you should have burning desire for it. Unless and until you don't have burning desire to be successful or to achieve that dream your action will be hollow and will lead you towards failure. The other important point to be thought carefully before proceeding further we have to distinguish between our wishes and desires because these terms are going to differentiate our real dreams from pipe dreams. Now if you want something may be a Car or a House or any other valuable but you don't have obsession to get the thing you want anyhow than it is mere a "wish".

On the other hand "Desire" is that emotional state of mind in which it becomes restless to get that thing which he had eye on it and ready to work relentless to get that thing. Among all human races, the child desire is incomparable because whenever children have desire of something, child uses all his might to get the thing and won't stop until child had it. It's a very challenging task to distract the kid from his desire. One should have such a burning desire for their dreams, goals and success. It is found that desire is one of the strongest emotions which compels human to come up with success in any undertaking.

A long while ago, there was king who was a great warrior. He came across the situation which prompted him to take the necessary decision to insure his success on the battlefield. He with his army was about to fight against the powerful king, whose men outnumbered his own. He loaded his soldiers into ships, sailed to the enemy's land, unloaded soldiers and equipment, and then he ordered his soldiers to burn all the ships which had brought them to this country. Addressing his men before the battle, he said "you see the ships have been turned down to ashes. That means we cannot leave this shores alive unless we win! We now have no choice either we win or we perish.

They won.

Every person who tastes victory in any endeavour must be willing to burn his ships and cut all his sources of retreat. Only by this simple act one can be sure of maintaining a state of mind called burning desire to win. You must learn that desire is the beginning form of everything man creates or acquire.

We have read the story of Dr. Sukhdeo shende in the first chapter, what prompted him to dream of becoming a Doctor is also an interesting story in itself. The boy had a dream of becoming doctor was backed by his burning desire which soon converted in to obsession, after he faced the criticism at school. At very young age of 12, one day he had severe cold due to which swelling in his nose aroused completely covering his whole right eye. Condition was so critical that he could not able to breathe properly. when he was taken to Dr. Dave after examining doctor recommended for immediate operation, which turned out to be successful and he returned home as a healthy boy.

Not even eight months have passed, he was again hospitalised for operation. When he was brought to the hospital, he was unconscious as he crashed in front of the hospital gates. Incident took place while he was climbing mango tree due to the stretch and pressure, his scrotnum got displaced into the inguivinal canal which left him with agony. It was second time he got operated by Dr. Dave. Just after six months of his operation his father got diagnosed with T.B and pneumonia. Doctor prescribed him take bed rest and started long medication course of 90 days. During this period the boy took great care of his father until he was out of the illness and ready to go for work. Not long after this incidence his younger sister while playing laid unconscious on the floor, as she got convulsion due to fits diagnosed by doctor.

This entire incidence had made influence over his mind, which lighted his inner flame of desire to become a doctor. So you can find in every other story of successful people like one of the doctor inscribed here, they have some strings of desire connected to their dreams or to become successful.

Dreams are like hot air balloon ready to fly, if fuelled by fire of desire or passion it will be overcoming the gravitational pull of obstacles. If you have burning desire to achieve your dream or to become successful, you can overcome any gravitational forces that are keeping you grounded away from your dream to fly higher and reach the heights. Positive thinking and motivation are the external forces but desire is more spiritual in nature, it comes from within. External forces cannot last long enough you have to feed your mind continuously with it but internal forces like desire doesn't need any drive to push you.

Arjun Mangal Shende had very humble beginnings in 1940. His parents passed away at the very early age when he was just ten, leaving behind one elder brother and one younger sister homeless on the streets. All three of them have to work in cigarette factory to keep their stomach full. Arjun was one of the creative in all three of them. He had willingness to learn and become poet but no schooling. One day while working he asked one of the factory worker "Friend can you just write my poem on this piece of paper as I don't know how to write? I may forget later if not jotted down on paper".

The co-worker replied "I cannot write for you, I don't have time for such worthless work". Arjun desire didn't let him stop over there he went on for several other people many times for months asking diligently for help but instead of helping him, they laughed at him, harassed him. Some of them even said "You belong to poverties state boy you should work hard to meet your needs rather than wandering into realm for dreams, it is impossible for an illiterates like you". The embarrassments made him more obsessed with his desire and he somehow managed to get into night school for 15 days to learn alphabets and how to make words from it. Later on because of his obsession to learn he read several books based on his fifteen days learning, placed himself in job with government, formed society for his community people. Till today at the age of 87 years he reads, writes his poems and trying to motivate other to do so. It was his desire which pushed him so far, motivated him to learn more. There was more internal motivation which moved him rather than external factors.

It is one of the common behaviour which is found major reason for failure, people not reaching their goals, not been able to accomplish their dreams is that people don't work with all their might putting their soul in it with all excitement and enthusiasm in the work they are suppose to do. Unless or until you don't have want of something so badly that it becomes a passion in your belly you won't able to make it till the end.

During the times of Socrates, one young man approached the great philosopher to know the secret of success. He humbly asked Socrates "What is the secret of success? Can you teach me so that I could become successful"? Socrates said to the gentleman "If you want to know the secret of success meet me tomorrow morning near to the river". As decided young man came to the spot told where Socrates was waiting for him.

Socrates said to man "Let's walk towards the river together".

They started walking and when they reached the middle of the river where water was up to their neck, Socrates to the astonishment of young man ducked him inside the water. The man struggled to be out of water but the Socrates was holding him with much strength sooner he started turning into blue. The young man struggled with all his might and finally got up to the surface gasping and taking deep breathes.

Socrates asked "When you were drowning down in water what did you want the most?"

The young man replied "Air".

Socrates said "Young man you had learned your lesson that is the important secret of success, when you want success as bad as you want breathe you will get it, there is no other way out".

Think long enough on the question why you want to achieve your dream? What are you truly seeking from life? Once you have clear conscience what your desires are? Then only you can design the tools in the workshop of thoughts by which you can build heavenly mansions of happiness, strength, success and peace.

Fun Activity to be practised:-

- Take a paper and write down all desirable things you want from life with valid reason which will lead you to sort out your actual dreams from pipe dreams.

Chapter – Three

"Imagination is the power house of all great Deeds – Ankit Shende"

Imagination is the place where the birth of the dreams takes place. Imagination is the Projector which runs the different dreams on the horizon of brain turning them into burning desire by rerunning the shows in our brain to generate the need so that it can become burning desire. For this reason it is important to know about our projector of brain.s

What Does Imagination means?

It means "The act of creating vivid pictures in mind". The person who understands the power of imagination will never take it for granted. It is the most powerful tool capable of writing your success story kept underprivileged. The reason why I said so and how it works is important to understand. The fact is our brain suffers from "perception of discord" which means it strongly dislike to hold two contradict beliefs at the same time and make it go nuts as much that it try to undermines the weaker belief and support the stronger one. When you're putting your imagination into work to see the glimpses of your success or dream, it activates your subconscious mind to visualize the picture of the future and then it compares with your present reality and it try to resolve the conflict by shifting gears from reality to your visualization to make it closer for comparison and drive conclusion from it. Therefore you have to hold on to your vision and keep imagining about it, this will make your mind to act like magnet to attract people, surroundings and information about your future. Every dream is having deeper roots of imagination.

Once the famous artist and sculptor Michel Angelo was asked "how do you carve and give such beautiful shapes to the stones to turn them into the scriptures?"

Michel said "Nothing! The statue was already there, I had just removed the unwanted part of stones".

The statue was present in stone is true but first it was in the mind of sculptor.

What I have observed that human are basically charged by thoughts and imagination, let us understand this with the small experiment which we have had came across once in lifetime in the childhood as means of play or fun activity or while reading science in our schooling days.

We will try it one more time to better understand it. Take a comb and paper. Tear off several bits of paper about the size of a pea or smaller and place them on a table or counter.

Next run the comb through your hair several times and again bring the comb near the bits of paper. What happens now?

What happens is that when you combed your hair, you gave the comb a charge of electricity and when you brought the comb near the paper bits, they were attracted to the comb because of this charge.

Likewise our thoughts and imagination plays the same role of charging us and attracting things, people and circumstance according to the frequency of our thoughts.

Negative thoughts and affliction which you are holding inside you is the biggest hurdle on your way to success and dreams. It is constantly charging you to attract the obstacle on your way, directing you to move towards failure.

Think of your mind as a mill whatever you feed into it, you will get finer output of it, like when you put wheat in the mill the output you get is flour but when you put pepper seed you can't expect to get flour as output definitely it will give you chilli powder only. Therefore when you feed your mind negative thought's you are churning out negative circumstances and surrounding out into your life. Even the lie detector has presented the fact, what we think our mind and whole body act accordingly. When you lie your heart beat increases, your hand try to sweat out, your body shivers from this you can calculate how much one negative or positive thought effect on you and your mind.

Our brain work on possibility of imagination, it does not really differentiate. This very act of brain is usually used or put to work in gym. In every gym they hang or paste different posters of bodybuilders in every corner of the gym with mirrors all round the workplace. When the person who regularly visit the gym for workout then his brain starts holding the images of poster hanged on wall and while working-out it makes comparison looking self in mirror to excel and to push forward.

From all the information gathered from various sources and experimentation researchers have derived conclusion that imagination has two elements one is primary and other is tertiary. Primary imagination is independent of facts, figures and laws we call it creativity. It cannot be binded and flies so vividly that even birds are poor match in flying to it. Various painter, writer, inventor, discoverer, leader, explorer are born out of primary imagination. They are men whose senses are alive, see opportunity and possibility where others see none. what would have happened today if group of scientist at Nasa was unable to see the possibility of going to the moon, what would have happened today if Thomas Edison had unable to see the opportunity where others had seen nothing then we would had never been able to discover the truth that man can walk on the moon or not able to live luxiourous life or would have led in darkness. The other is tertiary imagination often called accumulative imagination which is formed by storing of all the information which we gathered from books, observation, facts and our experiences through our life. To be successful we have to put forward our creative faculty instead of accumulative imagination.

Late Dr. Elmer Gates of Maryland was one of those scientists renowned for the very well use of primary imagination. He can be definitely categorised to the status of genius because of his interesting and significant method of using creative imagination. With engaging his creative imagination he had created more than 200 patents the evidence of which can be found in the United States patent office.

He had a unique laboratory in which he had a room called "Personal Communication Room". The room arrangement were with small table on which he kept his scribbling pad, pen and in front of the table on the wall was button to control the On/Off of light with room made practically sound proof. Whenever he was working on some project or invention, he would go into his room, make comfortable himself in his seat, put off the lights and focus upon the known factors of the invention remaining in that position until ideas begun to bump out of his mind on to the paper. On some occasion flow of ideas were so randomly that he would have to write for many hours and when thoughts stop popping out he would examined his notes with some known and some unknown facts, principles at that time. He made his living on it while working for some company or on some projects.

Self Help Assignment:-

- There is a simple technique which I practically applied to my negative thoughts and circumstances to get rid of it. The technique is to write down everything on paper, easiest way to free yourself from emotional pain, anger, anxiety and resentment. As soon as you write it down this feeling will relieve their grips on you. Take a paper and whenever a negative thought came to your mind write it down immediately and tear it apart and throw in dustbin.

- Gather all your family member and friends around you, declare them if I'm going to speak out any negative thoughts in front of anyone of you, charge me with treat to you at restaurant. Practise this activity with affirmation and soon you will find yourself free from every negative thought.

Fun Activity to be Practised:-

- To put your Imagination at work the exercise of vision board should given to you in first chapter should be practised.

- To increase the power of your creative imagination keep a drawing book with you and whenever you get time try to draw what comes into imagination. Remember don't try to imitate the surroundings on your drawing book.

Chapter – Four

"Believe you can and you're Halfway there – Theodore Roosevelt"

If "Dream is a seed" which is fuelled with "Desire to grow" then "believe is a fertile soil" on which it is sowed. It is important to know that without believe; it is merely not possible to achieve your dreams or to become successful. Believe is possibility of happening, it works wonder. Believe has the power to create dream or destroy it. Decades after decades things which you see around you was someone's dream and believe that it can be produce in the reality from aeroplane made by Wright brothers or telephone made by Graham Bell you use.

How believes comes from?

References are the source of believe or in other words we can say believe comes from references repeated day after day and "References" are all the experience you have observed, feeled and recorded in your nervous system, it can be your actual experience or imaginary (means only in imagination). Therefore every individual have different sets of believes as per his references, therefore it is important not to accept anything blindly because from time to time believes of people had changed whether at the time of Copernicus, when everyone believed that sun moves around the earth because anyone can stand at a point and see as the day passes by, position of the sun changes and eventually he can point out in the sky and say "See? The sun has moved from east to west" but in 1543 Copernicus challenged people believe and developed accurate model of solar system or at the times of roger banister in 1954 when people had imposing believe that no person can run a mile in four minute what they called "four minute mile". Roger not only challenged the peoples believe but started developing new believe of running a mile in less than four minute. In his imagination he had several time broken barrier of four minute a mile and repeating it several times in his imagination he provided enough references to strengthen his belief and produced result that was physically not possible for human being at that time and becoming first person to run mile in less than four minutes. After him he not only trained but also motivated several other youths to break it.

Let me illustrate you this with the wonderful gift given to us that is our brain where believe born and die. Brain have capacity and energy beyond our measures, it can accomplish any task we desire. Human brain works on feedback by nervous system, which is formed by billions of neurons also called nerve cells use to generate impulses. Neurons are crucial part of nervous system, it helps nervous system to interpret any information we received through sensory organs to convey it to the brain and to carry out instruction given through brain. Generally neurons act independently but they also communicate to each other through the medium of the nerve fibres. Therefore whenever we face a problem this neurons attack the problem all at once together. So whenever we imagine our dream for first time, we create a thin neural strand path which can be accessed again in future. Therefore every time we repeat the behaviour, the connection strengthens adding more strands to it finally building it into trunk line path of believe. The stronger is believe, the easier for you to forge your dreams into reality. Even the life survival of spider works on the principle of faith or believe to ambush its prey. Spider builds its web on faith that if any insect passes through it will get trap in the web. Think of when magnificent power of believe works wonder for small creature like spider what it can do for us. The deeper our faith is, the easier it is for us to achieve success.

First necessary step towards working on your dream is to believe in yourself and your abilities because "we become what we believe or think we are". Early from childhood we are programmed unknowingly in negative mindset more than positive suppressing our true capabilities. Child does everything without fear with passion, joy, excitement and carefree. If baby cries even the neighbours would know it or if baby wants something it will never let anybody sit quietly or if baby smiles, laugh it fills nearby whole surrounding with happiness. Child energy is always limitless but then adult start imposing their believe don't do that it is wrong, just beware of outside world it is unfair and so on making him/her grow into adult frightful. It can be understood well with the Fable of farmer and tiger cub. One day farmer was passing by the jungle to get to the other village to sell his farm products. While on the way he found an orphaned tiger cub resting under the shade of tree, he looked at baby tiger for a moment and continued his journey to the village. As an itinerary to be back to his home very next day, farmer goes on selling his farm products into the village. He started at dawn of the next day his way back to his home. While crossing through the forest, he found same baby tiger sitting under tree somber being lost. Farmer felt pity for him, he picked him up and said "Don't worry baby! From now onwards you will live with me. You are one special kind of dog". He brought him to his farm and kept him with other puppies in his farm. Soon becoming familiar to his environment cub started imitating the puppies. He grew up thinking he was a dog. He would bark like dog rather than roar, he trained himself to keep the watch and protect herds of sheep from jackal and hyenas.

Then one day tiger with other dogs walked to the bank of the river which flows with dense forest on the other side of the bank. He looked eagerly on the other side and wondered "What kind of animal is that? How brave, beautiful, graceful, powerful and free it is". Then he asked his fellow dog "What is that?" The dog replied "Oh, that is tiger but don't worry yourself about it because you will never be able to like that". The tiger came back to farm and continued behaving like dog. His believe never let him know the grand life he could have.

Time went on people came to know about the tiger who believe he is a dog, who behave like a dog and would come to have a look at him. One day a man came to farmer and said "I had heard it on the street about your tiger and had come to see whether tiger acting like a dog is true". Man knew that tiger is the Royal beast of the jungle but he was surprised to see the tiger playing with other dogs, barking like dog and keeping watch on sheep's. The farmer explained everything to the man that carnivorous animal is no longer a tiger. He has trained him from childhood to be a dog and now he believes he is a dog.

The man knew that there was more to this great animal than what his action showed and what he pretended to be a dog. He was born as a tiger, he had the heart of the tiger and nothing could change that. The man taken tiger to the end of the farm and removed the belt from his neck and said "you are the mighty and powerful tiger, go forth roar, chase the prey, hunt them down and live like a tiger". Tiger looked at man and then he glanced at his home among the dogs and sheep's where he was comfortable. He ran towards the home and continued doing what other dogs were doing. The farmer with content smile said "I told you it was a dog".

The man returned very next day and tried to convince the farmer and the tiger that, he was born to live a greater life. He took the tiger to the bank of the river and spoke to him "you are the mighty and powerful tiger. You belong to the jungle free and brave not for the farm. Stretch yourself go forth roar, chase the prey, hunt them down and live like a tiger". The giant beast looked at the man then again to his fellow dogs and ran towards farm.

Knowing facts about the tiger and what tiger are really about, man asked the farmer to let him try last time. He would return the next day and prove that this beast is a tiger. The farmer stated "otherwise it is a dog".

As agreed man returned very next morning to the farm and took the tiger and the farmer into the dense forest so that he could not able to see the farm nor the dogs and sheep's in the surrounding. Then man removed chain and belt from his neck and pointed towards the eye of fearful prey. He spoke "you are the mighty and powerful tiger. You belong to the jungle free and brave not for the farm. Stretch yourself go forth roar, chase the prey, hunt them down and live like a tiger". This time tiger stared at the prey and deep forest, stretched his body to make a stride and hunt down the prey. At first he moved slowly then massively, with mighty roar of the tiger.

Many times in your lives, you see and believe yourself as a dog following instruction manually given by the family, friends and people. You are not aware of your true potential grandeur. Other times you are going to drop down, crumpled and grounded into the dirt by the decisions you make and the circumstances that come your way. You feel as though you are worthless. But no matter what has happened or what will happen, you will never lose your value. You put layers of dust, crumpled yourself of past resentment, change yourself because of someone's opinion and end up losing your true self.

Believe can uplift or can put you in a trench, it depends totally on you what kind of believes you are carrying, and your mind will mould you accordingly. Long ago an owner of big toy Manufacturer Company decided to do the experiment; he gathered his entire worker in factory floor and divided them into two groups on the basis of their hair colour, black hair people and brown hair people. He told them I was going through a research journal published which says "The people with brown hairs are hard worker, intelligent, provide better quality and services".

Within a week the difference between black haired people and brown haired people had begun to be seen, the quality of work and services black haired people provide were continuously falling on the scale to the brown haired people. The brown haired people out performed in providing better quality and quantity in toy making.

Next day owner came and made an announcement; he said "I had made a big mistake. At the end of the research journal they had given conclusion, which tells the opposite story of what I had told you. They have concluded that black haired people are harder worker, intelligent, provide better quality and services.

Soon the result of the announcement was seen in the quality and quantity of work of the black haired people, they continuously improved to higher scales and people with brown hair started losing their rhythm and graded lower and lower on scale.

It was believe which was planted in their mind and result of which casted them out to degrade and outperform.

The next thing is never let yesterday's disappointments overshadow tomorrow's dreams because sooner or later those who win are the one who believe they can.

What would had happened when as a low boy, when Michael Jordan was cut from his high school team stop believing. We would have never able to hear the name of greatest NBA player of all time. After getting dropped from the school team Jordan didn't stopped he continued with his believe and trained himself intensely. His believe and work paid off, next year he made into the team in his senior year. Jordan foot got broken in the year 1985-86 but his believe of getting recovered and playing had given him fruit after a year in the 1986-87 season by becoming second player in the season to score 3000 points. He had missed more than 9000 shots, lost 300 games, 26 times not able to take the game winning shot, Instead of this also his believe was so strong that his success itself marched towards him in the form of numerous rewards. Jordan believes can be exemplified in his quote "You have to expect things of yourself before you can have them".

Faith is the foundation for every dreamer and successful person. The greater you faith is the greater the certainty of happening things. Many times life will test and challenge your faith but during those times it is you who will determine your fate according to your faith. Sylvester Stallone was a struggling actor and turned down by many producer to be given lead role of the movie but he continued with his believe of becoming a hero. After finishing his screenplay of his first film Rocky. Stallone met several producer who were ready to make movie from his screenplay but insisted to give the lead role of Rocky Balboa to other famous actor of that times such as James Caan, Ryan O' Neal and Burt Anderson but instead of compromising and settling down with low, Stallone walked away from all of them with his believe of taking a lead role. Finally he found Backers who were willing to finance with meagre budget of 1 million dollars. Stallone completed his shooting in just 28 days and Rocky went on for biggest hit on the screens in 1976 earning over 230 million dollars and it not only fetched him with Oscars for best picture and best director as well as acting and writing nominations also.

We should have faith unquestionably because it is the power of faith which does miracles. Believe in something whether God, Nature, dreams, yourself because believing gives you confidence to follow your heart. Your utter faith will always yield results. One such miracle happened long ago in a small village, when they faced an inevitable draught because village needs, flaura and fauna were fulfilled by rain water. Every year they had enough rain to fill their ponds, wells and to wet their fields for farming. This sudden draught made their fields go barren from the lack of rain. Ponds and wells were dried, village women had to walk miles into other village daily carrying their earthen pots for water required to fulfil their basic needs. Situation was irresistible as they were no signs of dark clouds which bring rain leaving people anxious and irritable as weeks turned into arid months with no sign of relief. The priests of the local churches called for an hour of prayer in village square on Sunday. They also insisted everyone to bring an object to show their faith in God.

Then on Sunday by evening square was crowded with people gathered with hopeful hearts for prayer. People brought variety of objects holy-books, flowers, crosses to show their faith in God.

By the end of prayer on magical commands it started drizzling. When people felt the soft rain on their skin soothing their soul, Wave of cheers swept in the crowd and they raised their objects of faith held high up in gratitude and praise. To everybody astonishment one faith symbol overshadowed all of them was a teenager boy brought an umbrella. When you do something in life, have complete faith that you will definitely succeed. Never do anything half-minded. Faith is a great foundation to build your life.

One very interesting fact has come forth through the researches done that our conscious mind works like captain of the ship guiding your subconscious mind. Subconscious mind doesn't differ in good or bad, true or false. Your subconscious mind just follows the order believing in your conscious mind reasoning faculty. Whatever your conscious mind gives information whether you say "I can't do it" or "I'm bad at it" or "I'm a champion" your subconscious mind does not question and believe it as truth and act accordingly. Late Dr. Esdaillea scotish surgeon in India used the power of placing believe in the subconscious mind during operations. During year 1843 to 1846 in Bengal he had done almost 400 different operations without the use of anaesthesia because at that time anaesthesia were not invented. He did this with the help of placing believe in the subconscious mind of patients that he is under sleep of anaesthesia. Practically you have also observed this if you had encountered some hypnotic expert. The person who is hypnotised does everything as per Hypnos specialist, if he says bitter gourd as banana order him to eat and tell the taste of it. The person surely eats it and reply "It is sweet" or if he tells him to walk or sit he does exactly the same because your subconscious mind controls your body. The example of it is when you are sleeping your all body activity works right from heartbeat to breathing. Adding to it which contribute to your believe is suggestions. All through your life from childhood till now people surrounding you like teachers, parents, friends and associate had contributed to negative suggestion campaigning making you think, feel and act according to what they want or to their advantage, to control you. Every school, offices had certain guidelines, rules and discipline to control you. Therefore to take control of your life where ever necessary, the best way is to feed your mind with Auto-suggestion, every time you hear a negative suggestion you have to firmly apply this technique replacing negativity like "You are weak" by "I'm strong enough to handle anything" conditioning your subconscious mind again and again. Even in the bible it is several time repeated "According to your faith is it done unto you". Therefore believe is key to unlock the wisdom and abundance of life.

Fun activity to be practised:-

- Stand in front of mirror daily ten times looking into the mirror your own reflection and say "I believe it's possible to have my dreams and nothing gonna stop me on my way."

Chapter – Five

"Decision Making & Goal Setting constitute your own personal GPS to success – Ankit Shende"

Practically man's life is shaped through power of decision. It is the moment of decision that everything happen in your life whether it is exciting or challenging or dull and depressed. Get into flashback of life, you will find that whatever today you are all because of decision you had taken. You had created and will create circumstances in your life by your decisions and once you catch up with this fact you can immediately change your circumstances and situation from where you are to where you want to be.

Decision making and goal setting are your own personal GPS global positioning system of your aeroplane heading towards your dream; it gives the direction and destination which helps you in organizing and getting disciplined so that you can arrive at your destiny without being misguided. Lack of anyone of them will only result in fall of your life plane emotionally, physically and mentally.

Every course of action you take in your day to day life is the result of decision making, right from reading a book or playing a sports or success in some endeavour. If you observe at level of scrutiny, decision making is influenced by two vital factors circumstances and change. Under what circumstances you are making decision which will bring necessary change in your environment is always the state of mind. Your frontal lobe of the brain evaluates the circumstances by two strong emotions of joy and pain. You have to take full responsibility that every challenge, happiness and affliction you are facing are the effects of your decision it is more like Newton's third Law every decision have equal reaction in your circumstance and life. You cannot control external factors like earthquakes, tsunamis, draught, epidemic or universal truth death neither any of us but you can change your life going through whatever circumstances maybe? They are like seasons always changing according to decisions.

Whenever your conscious mind gives feedback to your unconscious mind about your immediate environment it make decision according to it, suppose if you are going through some chaos in your life as soon as this information flows through your subconscious mind, your mind reasoning faculty starts evaluating its pros and cons and comes up with necessary solution for change in the form decision. For temporary solution in the form of short term beneficial decision or immediate response to change the environment or long term solution to overcome it. Your temporary decision of escape from chaos or immediate change is the reason for failure and for pain to resurface yet best decision is the decision of facing the challenges and overcoming it totally because it not only gives insight and experience but also helps you grow personally, spiritually and morally.

Another prospect is most of the time people don't do anything about their situation whether they are suffering from pain, some job they are unwillingly doing, there unhealthy relationship, there sinking business and lot more of it because of one simple reason that it will lead them to unknown and thinking "it's better to have something then nothing" never realizing this temporary decision lead there life to more misery and they are used by their own emotions never trying to experience other prospect of life which could pour immense happiness or new learning experience for them but if you want to be successful, you have to learn how to use your emotions of joy and pain for a change.

Every successful individual or company or nation had learnt this art and had used it to come up with decision which will bring success to their home. One of the greatest examples of it in our day today life is fortune five hundred companies endorsing their products through advertisement using people emotions and earning billions. Sometimes you not even know that they have compelled and used your emotion state whether you look at deodorant advertisement they endorsed there product that it will make you look desirable and let you attract opposite sex towards you or whether it is advertisement of soft drinks even some of you know they are harming because of their chemical contents but products is endorsed in such a way using emotional state that it will make you look cool, if you drink it or bring people closer or spread happiness result of which is you buy the product.

Next thing to put spotlight on the important habit of successful people which is cultivated by every successful person from past till present is that they are quick in making decisions and very slow in changing their decisions means once decision taken you have to follow with affirmation it should not be effected or influenced by external variables like peoples, circumstances but you can be flexible in approach of following your decision.

One such name was of Mr. Soichiro Honda founder of the Honda group of companies who had highly practised this habit. Mr. Honda had keen interest in automobile and auto-components. To support his interest he decided to open a workshop with all his wealth, he had so much affirmation about his decision and belief that he could develop auto-components which can be sold to Toyota motor corporation he betted all his money including his wife jewellery. While still in school, working in his workshop he developed the piston rings and presented before Toyota. Toyota rejected saying that it didn't meet the Toyota standards and he had to continue his schooling going through all bullying by faculty and fellow mates. Despite of this painful experience Mr. Honda firmly followed his decision and continue to work on his goal while changing his approach until he bagged the contract from Toyota after two years of labour.

But the messenger of misery didn't stopped here; soon Japanese government went on for war and refused to give him concrete which was necessary to build his factory. Mr. Honda with his team sticking to their decision came up with a solution for producing their own concrete and built their factory which was bombarded twice during the war destroying major portion of factory and gone through massive earthquake which levelled his factory. Than another problem arouse crisis hitting Japan badly due to war and scarcity of resources especially gasoline was faced all over Japan. Mr. Honda was also affected by it, he had to ride Bicycle even to buy grocery for his family. He came up with solution to attach motor to his Bicycle which was soon demanded by his neighbours. Within few weeks his motorized bike became so popular that he decided to open a plant but lacking of fund made him approach all bicycle stores in Japan to support his new invention which later opened the gate of Europe and America market for his invented motorbike followed by car in seventies outselling the Toyota. This all became possible due to one man's affirmation to truly follow his decision and never getting influenced by external environments.

Follow through of decision with affirmation is important. Almost 90% of the time we walked out of the decision made or sometimes in midway looking at circumstances but the fact is only the 10% time when we followed our decision has shaped our life till now. Another point to be noted is there are no such things like wrong or right decisions only different perspective. Now to understand my point think of two person standing facing each other on the two opposite corner of the table and in between them a coin is kept vertically standing asking question "what truth and characteristic they see in coin?" for one person head is the truth as he can see head side of the coin but for the other person standing opposite tail is the truth but we know both of them are true to their statement it is just about experiencing different reality. Similarly it is true for decisions also there are no right or wrong decision it is just about experiencing and learning different colours of life. Next thing to focus on is her twin sister "Goal Setting" they both work together holding hand in hand, when you have specific goal and affirm decision of working towards it then only success comes to your doorsteps. Now what does goal means? They are nothing but the dreams against ticking clock. Whenever you have a dream and you decide to achieve it within certain time frame then they are called as goals. According to me "Goals" are the "FAST" way of achieving your dreams where "FAST" means fire to achieve success against time. Goals are critically important like knowing the disease before taking the pills because the pills are off no good use if you have fever and you had taken the pills of digestion.

I came to understand about the importance of how we make decision and set desire goal from one of my childhood event which get recalled facing tough times recently. When I was low boy my father used to take both of us my brother and me every Sunday to nearby shopping centres and park for fun ride, entertainment and enjoyment. One of my father friend Sudhakar uncles had shop in the shopping centre of electronic gadgets and videogame parlour. Every time we visit uncle shop, we always keep checking with videogames, excited and played standing there for some time. Soon this habit turns into desire to have a videogame of our own so that we can play it at home. One day I demanded my father "Dad i want that videogame". Father politely replied "we can't but it now but sometimes later may be next year on your birthday I can gift you". But I already dreamed of it with strong desire for it, me along with my brother went on to uncle's shop and asked uncle "What is the price of videogame?" Uncle replied "Son cost of this videogame is 1600 rupees". When we came back home, we checked with our piggy bank saving we had only 200 bugs at that time. The question came how to fulfil desire? I and my brother were once clear with decision we will buy it anyhow and came up with plan to dad to achieve our goal. I said "Dad I want you to deposit daily 10 rupees in our piggy bank and in return we will promise not to go Sunday weekend fun trip, so that it will be equalize the money you spend every week for us". Dad nodded in yes with a smile.

Once our goal was set with time frame of five months, Dad and we started working towards it of depositing ten rupees in piggy bank and five month later we had our own videogame at home. What I learnt from my own personal experience is that if we set a goal, we are more able to recognize the things necessary to achieve our dersired objective rather than if we don't.

Every successful person has goals. It is absolutely necessary to have goal none of us can go simply driving on and on without knowing the destiny. Next thing is goal should be stamped with specific time frame because you are not somebody to leaves things on the chance or let become your dreams to be pipe dreams. Goals help you to organize, disciplined and will push you to limits to achieve. The best approach to it write down your goals against ticking clock, it is just as good as chewing your food 32 times before swallowing it. Goal can be for a day, a month, a year or years divide them into short term, medium term and long term goals.

One of my childhood friends Ashish was made to learn goal setting practise since school days by his parent. As a kid we don't know about the importance of goal setting and we use to spend whole noon till evening together and whenever i find his daily goal setting dairy i use to laugh but today it is very clear to me and him also that single habit made him more successful than any other of his batch mates and now he practise this habit by categorising it in two parts daily goal and long term goals. He had got working parents, so they cannot track down all the activity what their children are doing all day long at that time and as good parents they want their kids to be grown into healthy well being and respectable in the society. They came up with decision to make them into the habit of planning whole activity of day and when they are back from office they ask him and tell him to put tick before the goals achieved by him set by him for a day. His parents handed him with the dairy and before going to office they check his dairy what goals and objective he had made for today and at the end of the day how much objective he had accomplished out. This mere simple practise eventually turned into his habit and eventually into his success story at his job and relationship.

Fun activity to be practised:-

Decision making is more like other skill can be improved by practising, so here is the exercise for you practise it daily.

- Take a scribbling pad with you. Divide the page in 4 columns and write down what decision you made in whole day.

  1. Simple
  2. Personal
  3. Long term
  4. Immediate
  5. End Result (Possible outcome of it)
  6. Remarks (how can you improve it)

Practising this small activity will not only help you in improving your decision making capability but also keep you in check with your long term objective.

- Take a Drawing Sheet Divide it in three columns Short term goal(Quarterly), Medium term goal (Yearly) and Long term goal (Five yearly) and paste in wall or on the door of your wardrobe review it daily and put a tick mark when it is achieved.

Chapter – Six

"Explore beyond the realm of Fear for Unconditional growth – Ankit Shende"

Now the first roadblock comes along the way of success when you decide to start taking action is Fear. Although we are born with boundless energy and fearless. As a small baby we don't know what is possible for us or what is not? It is the limitation imposed into our mind by people around us and where this people get this believe from their forefathers becoming victim of victim growing into adult frightened without even knowing how much we can stretch or possibly what could be our own limitation is? Fear is not real, it is resistance prepared by our mind to talk out of things. I came to realization of the few facts about fear when I was in the meditation camp "Vipassana" questioning my inner self about fear. What I observe was interesting? I found that there are basically three states i.e. "Unknown, Pain and Loss" where mind generate resistance not only inside but also throughout the body sending impulses to react in opposition through every sensory organ. Next exciting disclosure which will raise your excitement level is that as soon as you step into your fear, start acting on it soon you will find it disappeared and your horizon automatically get expanded to reach your goals, to achieve the success or to fulfil your dreams. It is just like a caterpillar inside the cocoon which soon comes out breaking cocoon becoming beautiful butterfly more liberated and powerful to fly then earlier state of caterpillar crawling on hundreds of legs.

Once you know the cause you can overcome your fear with properly training your mind and discovering your new self potentially more potent than earlier. Let's dissect each of this cause in details. The first one is "Fear of unknown" it comes when your mind hits the state of unknown where it cannot derive conclusion more like the state of driving a car and meeting with a dead end ahead. To understand the "Fear of unknown" better let us put our thinking cap on and put ourselves into the situation discussed ahead. Suppose you are in a relationship with someone and you know that you are not happy with it but you still continue because of your mind cannot derive conclusion to question what will happen if I break the relationship?, What if the next relationship I move on to will be more punishing to me? Or what if I could not find somebody else and left alone? Or consider another situation suppose you have your exams very next day and you had studied two third of the syllabus still you will feel the fear until you don't have question paper in your hand because your mind inability to have meaningful answers to the questions like what will happen if didn't able to solve the question paper?, What will happen if I didn't able to clear the exams?, What will happen if I didn't able to finish it on time? Fear comes in the form of inner voice which will constantly ponder you. The only way to overcome it, Is to give it a shot. You will observe it as soon as you start facing it, pushing yourself beyond the realm of fear sooner or later it starts disappearing because earlier there was no such neural path in your brain for such activity and soon when brain your realises that it is not a dead end fear dissipates completely.

Next zone of fear is "Fear of Pain" your mind is conditioned to march you out from the pain and unpleasant circumstances. Mind had tendency to move toward the joy, happiness more therefore if it gets slightest clue that situation can also bring pain. Mind will resist with all might you can observe it in the form of inner voice continuously speaking "No I can't do it" or "No I will not be able to handle the outcomes" with body reaction changing in the form of different sensation. The vary example of it is some people having stage fear at that time state of mind is closely associated with painful references of facing criticism, embarrassment and harassment which could hurt their self image or suppose you have given important responsibility to handle a class of naughtorious student then this little voice inside murmurs "No I can't handle this job" or "No I can't handle this making fool out of myself" or suppose one of your friend who is little crook ask you to lend him some money but your mind try to speaks you out of the situation "No I can't handle if I'm being conned". The only way to come out off "Fear of Pain" is to face it again and again because this very act will make your mind comfortable with the situation and familiar with the outcomes. Every time when you practise the act it will make stronger neural path making mind to believe the outcomes can be handled. As soon as mind believes get stronger same task becomes piece of cake earlier from which it was afraid off. Changes the state of mind from I can't handle to I can handle much more than this.

The third state of fear is "Fear of Loss" it is natural form of the fear which consume our mind because it dwells on believe of mind seeking security from childhood to oldie. The fear of becoming old losing your youthfulness, fear of facing natural disaster, fear of losing financial security, fear of dying or fear of losing loved ones and many more but one must understand they are all part of change because as soon as you start accepting the fact that nothing is permanent you can live life in greater sense. We are afraid of losing that we have all the time that we clinched to it, holding on to it so tight that nobody can take it, hiding it from world but there is nothing we have ever achieved cannot lose in a blink of eye. We are so insecure and afraid of restarting our lives so we just carry on trying to sort out the currrent mess. We have to keep it in mind that whatever we make here, we have to leave here before leaving earth so let all be lost. Let them take away everything but as long as we have breathe in our nostrils, as long as our heart is beating, as long as blood is flowing in our veins we can create it back. We had done it earlier and we can do it again.

Now we are familiar with the "States of Fear", it's time to focus on where this fear dwells. We all have split personality one which supports positive changes brings success in life and other culprit one which shakes our confidence making us more fearful not letting us to do any task. To know ourselves in much better way and to get familiar with small little voice inside constantly murmuring let's conduct one experiment take few sketch pens of different colours black, blue, red, green, yellow and piece of paper to write. Now take the blue pen write on paper the word "Orange" put it down take another pen of colour black write on sheet "Green". Pick green pen inscribe the word "Red" on the paper now pick red pen write down "Yellow" similarly pick the yellow pen and write "Blue" on sheet of the paper. Put down your pen relax a bit, now look at the sheet and try to say the "Colour not the Word". What happened as you try to speak "colour" at the same time your inner voice murmured "word" throughout the experiment. This inner voice is expert in creating great deal of problems for us along the way of success. Next time whenever you hear this voice trying to pull you out of the work at hand, simply you have to just declare one phrase constantly till it shuts out "Out of my way, I have got to do this" and continue on your task. According to the research reports that more than 80% of the negative thoughts and worries which we carry due to fear never happen it means fear have less than 20% possibility of happening. This proof we all are winner on this front only we have to take measure against it, to completely undermine the fear.

Once we had all the information about what is the state of fear and where it dwells, we can overcome the fear slowly by taking action, by facing the circumstances from which we are afraid of, by conditioning our mind. We have nothing to do with fear just to know that it is present over there and work on the task from which we are fearful. It is just like the darkness and light, you can't do anything with darkness because darkness means absence of light similarly fear means absence of faith and confidence. Therefore to remove fear we have to focus and work on faith and confidence.

I would like to tell you the famous tale which has always given me strength over the fears for years is of Goliath and David. It started when philistine army declared war against the Israel. Both army gathered and camped on the opposite sides of a steep valley facing each other. Philistine army looked confident over there winning because of the giant name "Goliath". There was no match for Goliath in the battle field measuring over nine feet tall and wearing full armour. He came out of camp each day mocking and challenging the Israelis to fight but no one came forward. The king Saul and his whole army were terrified of Goliath. His fear has consumed so much in the hearts of Israelis that no one shown up for fight till 40 days until the day David came to the battlefield. He was sent by his father Jesse to bring back the news of his brother. He was young teenager boy. When he reached the camp, what he saw and heard was inacceptable for him. He heard from the other end of valley Goliath was shouting criticizing and challenging the Israelis and he saw the wave of fear stirring within the army of Israel. David fearlessly responded "Who you are philistine to defy the army of God's". To everyone astonishment David went to King Saul to let him fight against the giant, after little persuasion king agreed to let David fight against the Goliath. The army brought armour for David but he denied marched forward in his simple tunic, carrying simple staff, sling and a pouch full of stones. The Goliath began cursing him, hurling threats and insults with Philistine army laughing at his foolish act. To this David replied to philistine "Today you have done sin by defying the army of GOD, you come against me with sword and spear but I come against you in the name of almighty GOD. Today whole world will know that there is a GOD in Israel when I will give the carcasses of philistine to the birds of the air. The world will remember that not by sword or spear lord saves us because this battle is of lords and he will give all philistine into our hands.

Goliath moved to kill the David but within few reflexes David reached his bag picked up one stone and slung one of the stone to Goliath's head exactly finding the right space on his forehead permeating through the hole in the armour and he fell down on the ground. David then took Goliath's sword, killed him and then held his behalves head into the air. Philistine turned and ran when they looked brutal killing of Goliath their hero and hence forth Israelis chased them and defeated them.

David knew that if he conquered the fear his king's army will definitely defeat the philistine because everyone was fearful looking whole battle from Goliath points of view losing their confidence but only David looked it from other perspective thinking of Goliath as mortal man challenging the power of GOD. His act of courage and faith not only filled the confidence in Israelis but clearly made us also learn that if we can overcome fear we can endeavour anything irrespective of our shape and size of the problems.

Fun Activity to be Practised:-

- Gather you friend and family members at least once in a week in a garden or open place to play truth and dare game this is the best therapy to overcome fear. I know this sound awkward and childish to many of us but trust me you will learn to overcome fear with fun and happiness.
- Make a list of things you are feared off and step into them like if you are having stage fear try to perform as many times as on stage until your neural path become strong and fearless to face it.

Chapter – Seven

"Actions are the genric source of success – Ankit Shende"

Dreaming and believing is not sufficient for the success. These are the only way to equip yourself with the necessary ammo and armoury for your battle. They are not the process; it will start when you start acting on your dreams, taking action or steps towards the success. Deer itself never enters the stomach of sleeping Lion, infact he have to hunt him down likewise only dreaming and believing will not work we have to start acting on it.

Once a well known speaker who started his seminar by holding up a 1000 Rupees Note. In the room of 200 people, he asked, "who would like to have this 1000 Rupees Note?" Hands started going up. He said, "I am going to give this note to only one of you, who is more deserving for this."

He proceeded to every row in the room with hand held up above waving the 1000 Rupees Note. He then asked, "Who wants it?" Still, the hands were up in the air. Reaching back to the stage and standing there he replied. "What if I raise the bar by 1000 more? Now who wants more?" Still the hands went into the air but out of 200 one came from back to the stage and took the money from his hand.

Speaker continued his speaking and said "My friends, you all learned a very valuable lesson. Some of you believe that you deserve this 2000 Rupees, some dreamed of it but the truth is that the person among you who took action towards it was the one who got it". Likewise most of the time in life we have the ideas, dreams upon which we never acted, other times we believed we will succeed but never took that one necessary step towards it of "Action".

It should be absolutely clear; to shape your life is to get yourself to take actions. Actions will put you into the motion which will ultimately lead you to your destiny. Every one of us has noticed that when we go to a restaurant first we order and eat food then only we pay the bills but in real life where nature law follows is vice versa first we have to give or take that necessary action then only we can reap the success.

You have to also keep it in mind that not every action will lead you to success. Therefore, we should become familiar with what kind of action can soar us to the heights of success? Explanation to this question goes with the story of three men who were close friends. One day all three of them were going through the fields observed few men riding the horses and doing some acrobats with horses. They all got excited when they hit the stable because deep inside they had the strong desire to ride horse like the men on the field. Although the first man had deep desire to ride the horse but he stood still near one of the horse filled with fear of falling from the horse and getting hurt not even trying to climb on his back. The second was brave one without even thinking he climbed up on the back of the horse and fallen down while riding few feet ahead getting his back hurted, fractured right arm and wounded both knees concluding his journey never to try again with fear of falling consuming in his heart. The third one was the wisest of them all he went to the field first, then asked one the man who was riding the horse, how to ride it and learnt the art properly from it for few hours and then he tried running the horse on the fields. When he got enough confidence then he tried acrobats with it fulfilling his desire.

The real purpose of telling this story was to give you insight of the three paths out of which only one leads to success. Those three paths are thinking without taking action, taking action without thinking and the path of taking action with thinking and learning. The path of thinking without taking action was taken by the first person in whom he had strong desire for his dream but never took action because of the fear which made him failure. Most of the time people set out goals have dreams with strong desire for accomplishment to attain true happiness but never took the necessary step towards it making them by default failure due to procrastination, fear and setbacks. The next path is of the taking action without thinking which is more dangerous and also lead to the failure as followed by second person of the story. Practically in life most of the people fall trap on to this path taking action without thinking. The best example to look around are the people in your circle who started some business and failed losing their money not even realising that before starting anything you have to gather all the information and learning about it. Finally the path which leads to success is always the one taking action with proper thinking and learning the necessary skills to start with process which the third person took in the story. First gathering all the information about it, then learning the skills, getting training on the skills and then taking the action which will definitely bring success in whatever endeavour set before them.

Once we know how and what kind of action is required we are on the track of success. Long ago a wealthy businessman bought an expensive luxurious car but after few days car engine failed and businessman called experts to fix the issue. One after another many experts visited and tried to figure out the reason of failure to fix it but none of them succeeded. The owner of car than brought one experienced old man who was expert in fixing the problem of such luxurious car.

The old man along with his tool box reached the place where car was parked. He went on for inspection in front of the owner itself after carefully inspection he took out the small hammer from his tool box and tapped at one portion of the engine. Instantly engine started and he kept his hammer back into the toolbox as engine was fixed.

The owner asked the old man "How much I have to pay?"

The old man handed him with a bill of ten thousand rupees which shocked the owner and he exclaimed "for what this much amount you had hardly done anything?"

The old man replied "One hundred rupees for tapping the hammer and rest nine thousand nine hundred for where to tap". Therefore taking action is important but right direction and what kind of action required is going to make all the difference. Before taking action we should be aware of the pros and cons of the step we are taking, complete knowledge about it is more important than only we can drive home success.

Fun Activity to be Practised:-

- Play solving Rubik cube because it requires thinking with action and also learning to solve the cube fully.
- Try to solve puzzles this will increase your ability to take action with proper thinking.
- In Goal chapter you had defined your goals on a drawing sheet now it's Time to work on them take a scribbling pad and first research how you will proceed to achieve those goals and then start taking action towards it.

Chapter – Eight

"Money is a Tool use it wisely – Ankit Shende"

Most people make a mistake that creating a plateau of money as a dream but one should come to clear state of mind, money is just a building tool for the life of your dreams. Money is like fragnance, spread it! It will make surrounding happier but if you stock it up it will rot.

The question comes in mind why I said so? To understand it better let's take a situation suppose you are given huge amount of money with restriction that you cannot spend single penny from it. In such situation you will come to realization that dream of acquiring piles of money looks as futile as having best candy in the world in your hand and never eating it. It is the power off purchasing that it poses attracts you. You want money to fill your life with things that you think can bring happiness to you, what you dreamed off? The living standard you think you deserve. We all learnt important lesson in our school from well known story of "Midas Touch" in which king asked for one wish to convert everything he touch into gold from god and he was granted with wish, what happened next everybody knows it very well he ended up abruptly converting his own daughter into gold and finally understanding the importance and true purpose of gold. As we grew up we forget this important lesson isn't it but even today fact have never changed and will never change.

One of my friend shoeb came to realisation about dream of earning piles of money is never can be true dream. When he was on the job of software developer and was at the top of his performance in his company, travelling to different European countries, got a paid hike to double his package. He was having everything till that point of time but sooner all this success became meaningless as when he looked into his day today life closely that what he was doing boxed in routine of office to home and then back to office just to stock more and more money never truly spending more than his needs and enjoying true riches of life. Suddenly one day he questioned himself "Now I had all that money which I dreamed off but why I'm not happy?"

One single question cleared all his thought that money cannot be true happiness, he is just into the trap of never ending rat race and actual happiness stays within the work we want to do, the contribution we want to do society, sharing happiness and moments of joy with our family, friends and relatives and the real dreams are not in possessing lot of valuable materialistic things and money but in an intangible things which he wants to do in life. After that he quitted his job and went for what he really wanted to do in life to be a musician, earned a grade certificate from Trinity college of London in classical guitaring. Now he is taking classes and performs in local shows living a content, much fulfilled and happier life.

We are living in such an era where money is the only single subject which is highly linked to our emotional state of happiness and pain. Importance of money is so deeply rooted in everyone's belief that it is used as measuring standard for quality of life you are living, a source of freedom, power, security, pride. Some even relate money to success, if you have earn piles of money then you're are successful and if you are not having enough money that means you lack critical resources in life. Nobody can deny that money is one of those things which affect our day to day life. Our believes about money has become so much robust that we had chained it's scarcity to our emotional state of anxiety, frustration, fear, insecurity, worry, anger, humiliation and overwhelmed which ultimately brings pain to us. We are so blinded by our faith that we believe, if we had enough money all challenges of life would dissipate but it's not true. You cannot kick cancer out of the body by having money yet it can only help you get services like caretaker, chemotherapy. Money cannot make your kid educated it can only provide services like school, tuitions, books. It cannot make love to your spouse but it can provide medium to express your feelings of love to your spouse in the form of gems and jewellery. I had given you all the evidences to make it clear that "money is just a medium of exchange" from ancient time it is used for transferring valuable and sharing services with society called bartering. Remember material happiness never last longer, it just give you happiness for a moment. After a while you will feel lousy again and urge to have next thing which you think will make you happy.

If you run after money it is a terrible master bringing greatest chaos to your life and will keep you on your knees down in worst kind of slavery vice versa if you choose money to work for you there is not excellent servant then money. As a servant it works relentless day and night. Money has not only worked as great and faithful servant for individuals but for companies and nations as well. The distinguished example of it is Japan. Japan is now one of the world's dominant power economies. After war Japanese industries were almost ruined, it was Mac Arthur Japanese general who called Dr. W. Edwards Deming in 1950 and appointed this American quality expert. Deming started training Japanese with his principle of qualities. The theme of which is the belief of providing never ending commitment to increase the quality of services and work they are providing termed as Kaizen. Within few years this commitment started giving fruits by flooding world market with Japanese products and services making Japanese play major role in the world economy. Small decision of Mac Arthur investing money in employing Deming changed the whole economy of Japan. Today every year in Japan Demings Day is celebrated for giving such important wisdom. Yet financial independence is important for everyone but one should learn from Japanese example that "money is equals to valuable" means medium of exchange that is if you want to have money you have to provide something valuable in return. When this formula worked for the whole nation why not for individual like us. The only secret to gain financial freedom or have more wealth is to be "more valuable" whatever it may be either in terms of services, skills or products. For example an engineer is always paid more than a labourer because he had worked hard and developed himself enough that he will be more valuable to people then a labourer. It can understood as a method to devised to add real values to other people's life or the ability to convert which is very little in value to something significantly greater in value for others and this will open the door of abundance wealth for you. The only reason why most people don't do well financially is that they believe to get something for nothing or to growth in income without giving more contribution to company or society.

Another example which I came across that money is terrible master when my mother Dr. Jyotsna Mhaskar Shende was going through up's and downs of the business. She had gone through tough time while running her nursing home when 17 gynaecologist where working in a small town of radius 10 kilometres sparsely populated. Out of 17 Doctors 15 of them started doing scissors even if pregnant women can deliver normal baby in greed of earning more money but my mother kept here ethics and commitment of giving more valuable or contributing more to people's by trying to do more normal deliveries. As a result those 15 Doctors, who looked for short term gain and greed of money, were soon out of business because they were driven by money. Therefore if you want to attract more wealth you have to contribute more. We should never worry about money because as soon as we increase our skills and started contributing more eventually money comes to us. We should more importantly focus on learning not earning which will eventually lead us to earning.

Tanushree Goyal from Rajasthan India presented another great example if you have got skills and ready to provide services to community, money will follow you. She was in class 12 when she made her first social project for the villagers who lived nearby Jaipur city. Tanushree made her community project according to the needs of the villagers. She created an online store to buy and sell fresh vegetables which connected several farmers and consumers directly to meet their end needs. It was result of her labour for 3 years which helped farmers to raise their productivity and consumers getting their needs fulfilled although she was not paid for this project and services provided.

But in year 2015 her past labour and services provided opened the opportunity for even bigger horizon for her career with money following her. On the basis of her previous project success she was offered 300,000 dollars scholarship along with full paid accommodation, insurance and other expenses to study in Columbia University in stream International Issues and Political science. Therefore remember money is only medium of exchange so if you think you should get more money for nothing it is impossible with money. If you want more money you have to provide something equivalent back to community in any form. Another point to be noticed is money is only a building tool to achieve one's objective and success.

Fun Activity to be Practised:-

- Try to provide services or small help to your family members, friends and neighbours at least once in a week and make a note of it to develop a habit.

Chapter – Nine

"To be Successful become Self centred not selfish – Ankit Shende"

Most people can be found complaining around us "They too had big dreams with strong desire and believe in themselves and their dreams but they could not succeed even though they had taken necessary steps towards it". Then they think people who attain success in making big dreams into reality are the lucky ones. But in reality all these reason are false because the real reason behind the scenes is they missed the key note of focus while playing. When you have dreams with strong desire and believe to attain them. Even if you had started acting on it you will not succeed until or unless you are not working single minded. This thought can be well supported International renowned tennis star Venus Williams who once said "I don't focus on what I'm up against, I focus on my goals and I try to ignore the rest" you have to be just like that. Venus Williams had won two gold medals in Olympics and seven singles grand slam titles. Once you have came to know about the missing quality while working the next question comes why it is important to focus? For answer let's put spotlight on race horses. You must have seen race horses either on television, some movies or on the fields to the scrutiny you will find Race horse are always made to wear blinkers hood sometimes known as blinders. Blinders are a piece of horse tack that prevents the horse from seeing to the rear and to the side. It keeps horse to be focused on Race track and winning ribbon encouraging him to pay attention to the race rather than other distractions.

It is necessary to become self centred while running on the tracks of the success or your dreams. It is like wearing the blinders which will keep you on Track and not to be distracted by secondary activity. If you are not self centred you will be easily influenced by external factors like people, emails, social media and obstacles, chances are there you will be convinced to talk out of your way.

We are into electronic and computers generation, where there are plenty of distraction in our daily life from ringing phone, email notifications, twitter and facebook affecting our quality of work. They urge us to get connected to stream of information coming our way. To pay more attention to communicate and consume information rather than to focus on actual work. We cannot deny the advantage of being connected to people through social media when we need break from working long hours to rejuvenate our working levels and stress free our mind. Therefore we have to maintain a balance between work and distraction it is just like when an athlete make sprints during his practise sessions with small intervals to revital his body, to come up with normal breathing from gasping, to let his body cool from pressures of high temperatures. Similarly if we divide our working hours with short gaps for distraction it will not only refreshes our mind, release stress but also helps develop creativity at work. More often this has happened with everyone of us while working for long hours on some problem our creativity get clogged in one directional thinking only but when we take short break go for some refreshment, distraction and suddenly we get striking at head with brilliant solutions to the problem.

Being connected through various distractions of social media like facebook, twitter gives instant pleasure by overlooking the long term negative consequences. When we do certain distraction activity, it gives us instant positive response which adds to our level of joy stimulating our brain to excess more of it. This is the reason why we are becoming addictive to being connected and distracted but if we want to produce astonishing results, we have to learn the art of focussing when we focus all our efforts on one task or skill or work the results which change to much higher scale from previous results.

If you focus on something despite of challenges faced you can achieve it was very well understood by the Lionel Messi. As a low boy he had been diagnose with hormonal problem which affected his growth and his parents were not able to afford the expense of medical treatment for him. Although they tried with various wealthiest teams to pay for the bills of their talented young boy but all they had to leave bare handed. Messi was determined to make his career as a footballer so he didn't focus on his weakness and defects rather he focused all his energy on his strength, improving skills and on his goal. he was not ready to accept being defeated he crossed the Atlantic for trials in Barcelona. Looking at his great football skills Catalan Scout signed him for team and assured him that they are going to pay for his medical treatment.

He was the youngest player to play in international club matches at the age of 17. Later he won the fifa player of the year award and also registering his name in the list of world's richest footballer. Lionel Messi had humble beginnings but he not only overcame his physical deficiency rather he also turned his short leg deficiency into his advantage of quick change in direction and great balance on the field with the power of concentration.

Next fact to grip in with is until or unless you don't become self centred, you cannot connect with your inner genius and will fall in the trap of the competition, which itself means second class. Competition makes you compare your self-worth with someone else as measuring standards and you degrade your self-worth, never reaching your true potentials. It only makes you follower rather than leader. When you are not self centred you will merely distracted what others are doing? You will try to follow them which is not healthy for your success.

Once you become self centred you will able to focus on things which you want in life. Focus means "concentration in any form" which is an amazing phenomenon. When I was at the age of 12 years the science experiments left me spell bound when my elder brother ignited a piece of paper with by focusing the sun rays on the paper with the help of magnifying glass but same rays when concentrated and passed through prism make it dispersed into seven different colours were shown like a rainbow. Our own efforts, energy and time are like sun's rays when we focus all of it in one direction we get what we want out of life but if you become selfish or put it in wrong direction it will burn every essence of life and happiness around you like rays concentrated through magnifying glass. It should be more focused on your dream like rays on to the prism you will get what you have desire and dreamed off with long lasting contentment, happiness and your luminousness will spread around like rainbow with seven colours.

Fun Activity to be Practised:-

- Play a game of chess with any of your friends and family member it definitely increases your ability to focus.
- Meditate in calm and quiet place at least for half an hour.

Chapter – Ten

"Your level of commitment determines the quality of the life you are going to live – Ankit Shende"

Commitment is one of the strongest pillar on which the foundation of dreams are to be kept. If you have strong desire to fulfil your dreams in prescribe time limit with believe in your abilities and your dreams for which you have started taking necessary steps with keeping constant focus on your target than you have to hold "Commitment within your heart" that no matter whatever may be circumstances you will not walk out of it until you get the desired outcome because people those who taste the deserts of success are the ones who are totally committed. Few months back only I was invited by two of my favourite college juniors Puneet Saxena and Mohit Gupta on the occasion of successful completion of five years of their company with recent achievement of expansion of their company bagging bigger projects. They had started company in 2009 with borrowing money on high interest rate as much as 10% per month undergoing through all sorts of troubles we can imagine from people critics, comments to ups and downs of the business and competition. While congratulating them I promptly asked them "How did you accomplish such a great victory by taking your business to such a heights?" they said in unison "It was our total commitment to our dreams" heard the least expected answer because most of the people like them when asked similar question about success had reluctantly given the answers like the secret behind our success was our believe in our abilities and dreams or hard work or determination or capability to take risk and so on. Before application of "Total Commitment" first we must become aware of it.

To come to awareness about "Total Commitment" let's go through a parable of two close friends Rohit and Shobhit illustrating the total commitment. Rohit and Shobhit both had keen interest towards music with long held desire to learn and play guitar in the cultural event of the college fest. One day sitting on the bench in the park Rohit told Shobhit about his willingness to learn and play guitar in an event. Shobhit said to Rohit "I too had same dream as you friend" finding common ground they flared to fulfil their desire by deciding to take classes and to play guitar in an upcoming cultural event. Therefore keeping their goal in focus they started working on it by taking classes but eventually after some classes Shobhit started skipping classes and practise due to inconvenience while Rohit kept on continuing despite of everything. By the end of the year Rohit played at cultural event fulfilling his dream with rewards of happiness, appreciation and applauses while Shobhit was seated among the audience with regrets.

Now the question comes why this happened? Although both had same dream with strong desire, well defined goal with focus on it, even they had started working on it than also only Rohit was able to succeed to attain his goal. The answer to this question is Shobhit was just interested in learning and playing guitar because when we are interested in doing something, we proceed in that direction until when breeze is in favor of us means till the situation is comfortable. Shobhit also walked out of it once he started facing inconvenience. On the other hand Rohit was "Totally Committed" which means doing something until expectation is not met with "No non-sense" attitude. When the person is totally committed, he/she will not differ from its path even if circumstances are not favorable till the desire results is not achieved.

Next point is, it is absolutely true "your level of commitment determines the quality of life you are going to live". Many people underestimate the power of commitment and end up living life of mediocre. Commitment varies in depth that is why I used the word "Total" with commitment now let's understand the science of real and fake commitment. Real commitment brings changes which are long and lasting while fake commitment is always resistant to change with lots of doubts and questions, they often have justification for their limited actions. People those who are really committed have strong supportive reason for doing something with persistence in their action even if they face adversity. They follow their principles, values and belief because it's the emotional influence when people move away from their goals most of the time. Really committed peoples had no doubt about what is to be done?

One such person who marked his name in the pages of history was Washington with his Unfailable commitment overcoming the most challenging circumstances one can face and setting the example for upcoming generation. In 1883 it was just a creative dream which popped up in head of John Roebling to build a spectacular bridge connecting Newyork city with long Islands. Roebling enthusiastically went on discussing his dream of building bridge with experts throughout the world but had to face disappointment with people finding it not feasible and practical to build such bridge.

Roebling know his dream was not in vague even though people said "It was Impossible to build such giant bridge, you had to forget your dream". Roebling was not discouraged with such critics and comments Instead he knew deep inside that people were lacking the vision which he could see. He was so occupied by his vision of building the bridge that he thought about it all the time. Sooner he became so obsessed about his dream that his heart completely filled with belief of it can be made. Therefore he didn't stop and kept on sharing his dreams with other people after many rejections finally Roebling succeeded in persuading his son Washington that bridge can be built. Washington was an engineer.

Once Washington was convinced, both of them started working on the concepts of bridge, how such great structure can be built? What are the challenges before them? And how to overcome any obstacles and tackle the problems that will arouse while working? When they had prepared their proper blueprint and plan of action, they began building their dream bridge with passion marching their crew members for work. The project took off the ground very well while few months passed when project was underway a tragic accident happened on the construction site which took the life of John Roebling and left Washington bedridden for lifetime paralysing every part of the body and not been able to talk.

Negativity filled the air amongst the people along with comments from them "We told them don't be crazy about chasing such a wild dreams, it can't be done". Sooner people lost their hopes and felt that project is now scrapped because Roebling only knew how to build this bridge. Despite of being bedridden Washington faith in building the bridge was not been moved even an inch. He was not discouraged and still had the burning desire to complete the bridge. He tried to inspire and motivate his friends by conveying his message that it can be built but every one of them was deflated in their spirit and afraid of incident that took place. Washington was not a man who would have give up in the hands of his circumstances. He overcame this challenge with his only finger working in his whole body. He decided to make best use of it by developing a code language to talk to his wife. Whenever he had to convey message he touched his wife's arm and try to write or explain his message through code.

Later on he used his new developed sign language with his wife to call engineers back to work and instructed them how to proceed further as a result of which project started again. It took thirteen years for Washington to complete the bridge which he along with his father had dreamed off. During all those year it was her wife who carried out and conveyed his instructions given by Washington tapping his finger on his wife's arm. Today world knows the renowned, spectacular and magnificent Brooklyn Bridge as the winning glory of one man's total commitment along with patience and love of his wife who were not ready to give-up under any circumstances.

Fun Activity to be Practised:-

- Funny thing about commitment we all make shallow commitment every New Year taking resolution therefore now time has come to renew our resolution and start connecting for task which we had taken resolution.

Chapter – Eleven

"Add a little regularly to make it a whole – Ankit Shende"

The phrase "Add a little regularly to make it a whole" speaks volume. Success and greatness is never hammered out in a single day but working persistently day after day. Take one step at a time and think of it as marathon not a stride. Sachin Tendulkar made a world record of 34000 runs and hundred centuries not in a single day but gradually working each day towards his goal of achieving excellence in his craft and result of striving towards excellence in his craft is the reward of world record.

Pick up any ancient success story book or history of Iconic person you will find that every success has the strong foundation of being excellent in the craft you have been doing, you have to work single minded whether it was Arjun from great Indian mythology Mahabharata he perfected his skills so well that he can hit the eye of fish revolving above just looking into the water or whether it was Prithviraj chauhan of 11th century who had mastered the art of archery to hit the target by calculation of distance and location of his target from the words of poet or whether its 20th century Pele or Maridona who outshined among other players as player of the century because they all have one thing in common to achieve their dreams, goals they worked persistently on mastering the art by making it their habit to achieve excellence.

This is the key quality which should be developed by everyone to be successful in an endeavour because your success is always the measure of the number of hours you have given to achieve it. It can be validated with mark sheets we had got in school class and colleges, our grades are equivalent to our efforts most of the time. Many players who were with Michael Jordan in an Olympic team reported while they were on practise sessions with Jordan. He was always the first one to enter the floor and last one to leave the floor. Therefore it was evident the boy who was dropped out of high school team because of his low level skills and short height later made into the world class basketball player. The reason was his persistence to work towards mastering his skills which he turned into his habit by working day in and day out.

Once you set your goal, started working on it with focus and commitment to let no idea go until it comes to fruition than only quality required is to work persistently day in and day out until it become part of you, until you develop a habit because the longer you hang in there despite what comes your way the greater are the chances that thing will happen in your favour, the greater will be your success.

Long back Henry Ford decided to produce V-8 motor engine. He called his team of an engineer and told his vision about the engine than he instructed them to design an engine. After few days of working engineers come back to Mr. Ford with design on paper and reported "Mr. Ford it was impossible to cast entire eight cylinders into one piece of block".

Ford said them "Go back and produce it anyway" to this engineers replied "It is impossible to cast such engine" but Ford somewhere had believe deep down that if we workout persistently, it will drive results so he ordered them firmly "No matter how long it takes or how you do it? Stay on job until you get it done". The engineers went back to work because they knew, they had no option either they will loose their job or they had to give it a shot. Six months passed on in a fly preparing several plans to cast the engine but still no progress. Another six months passed with failures in attempt and task still seems impossible to them. Ford went on to check with his team of engineers assigned for project to know the progress and again he was informed by the engineers "There seems to be no solution to carry out the task to come up with results".

Looking to the gravity of situation and discouraged engineers Ford again commanded them "Keep on working until you succeed because I want it anyhow". Engineers went back to work and finally they discovered the way to do it. Therefore it is evident if you have dreams along with strong faith and deep desire back by total commitment to stick to the task until you get the desire results will definitely reward you with success. We all should agree for success action is required but more important is persistence to follow the course of action every day making it the part of your routine without getting influenced by circumstances and always finding way to continue with innovation, creativity brings success.

Another point to be focused is to improve and try to perform better than your previous work performances, to improve your ability and skills. Every step you make to achieve your goal should be better than previous step than you will not only have excellence in your field but will also have success at your feet.

Bruce lee was the legend of martial art he had routine of running three miles a day with good pace. On an average he would run a mile with a speed of six to seven minutes a mile. His friend also joins him on his fitness regime.

One morning he said to his friend "Today we are going to run five miles". Little bit anxious with his words, his friend said to lee "I can't go for five, I'm too old for it" and for few minutes he fumbled all kind of excuses in front of lee to not to run five miles. Bruce said "Daily we go for three; it's easy only two more and I know you will do it". After a pause his friend nodded his head saying "Let's go for it". They ran three mile and when they were on the fourth, nearly half a mile had passed his friend began to gasp with heart pounding like it will be out anytime he said "Bruce I can't go anymore and if I ran further, I will have heart attack and going to die". To this Bruce replied "Than Die!" hearing such exclamation his friend got nuts and ran full five miles. Later on he went to Bruce to ask "Why did he say so?"

Bruce said "You must have died either but seriously if you always put limits on what you can do physically or mentally, it will spread like plague into rest part of your life. It will spread its wings into your work, morality, your entire being. There are no limits what we can do rather we can think them of as plateaus you must not stay there infact try to go beyond them even if it kills you. A man must constantly try to exceed his levels and limits".

Fun Activity to be Practised:-

- The only time where we can induce the task in our habit is following the procedure for 21 days continuously and the best time to set reminder in our clock is at the time of taking our meals.

Chapter – Twelve

"I have done lot of Mistakes yet one more to create a Milestone of success – Ankit Shende"

Once you start acting on your goals persistently to achieve success you are going to make mistake along the way, mistakes are inevitable. This is where many people going to give-up on their goals, dreams because they are not prepared to mistake while working on their goals to bring home success. Now if we split the word in two, what we get out is "Mis" and "Take" therefore word mistake itself represents the thought that we have missed the appropriate or right action towards the desired objective.

I believe in making mistakes because when you pile up all your mistakes and look at the level of scrutiny you will find that they are your experiences. As well said by Oscar Wilde "Experience is the name given to the mistakes".

Let's go quickly back into the flashes of memory of past life and tell me "You had not done any mistake in your life". Yet no one is out there who can come up with the answer that they are flawless, everybody makes mistakes in this world whether it's personal, professional or social. Ok! Now let's check by shortening the time span to a week go back and try to recall what mistake you had done within a week like missing a phone call, skipping a meal, stabbing your toe or arriving late.

When you start recalling you will come up with a long list of mistakes. Therefore what we can conclude is that mistake is both natural and vital part of life.

I believe that we all make mistakes in life to learn from them but we can learn only from mistake when we admit it that we had made a mistake because if we blame others or the nature of mistake, we will miss the opportunity of learning any lesson from it. Blaming others is an act of cowardness it will leave us far behind on the course of growing and developing our innate capabilities or potentials but if we act courageously accepting our mistake, taking full responsibility towards it we open the door of progress and achieving desired results.

Weed of becoming best at everything is highly cultivated almost in the mind of every individual making no room for mistakes. It is being taught and highly practised in our school, family, society or at work place to feel guilty about mistake and try to avoid it as much as possible but on the other hand successful people take positive attitude towards the mistake.

I came across one such phrase said by a Businessman "Anything worth doing well is worth doing badly in the beginning". All of us will have to admit it and have experienced throughout our life what he said is true. Take a flashback into the memories of old days when you first learned to drive a car, to ride a bicycle, to play an instrument or to play a sport you were having a clear mindset in advance that you are going to bad at it first but gradually you are going to make the progress. You know the awkwardness is the part of it while learning the new skill.

Observe the baby when it try to start walking, Baby falls and stumbles many times but neither his parents nor baby stop themselves due to this awkwardness, so you have to be willing to go through that awkwardness to become proficient. As a child we give ourselves permission to go through mistakes, awkwardness and learn from it but as we become adult, we are so often afraid of making a mistake and never try to learn as children do.

We should feed our mind that when we walk on the path of success which starts with making mistake and improving it, once we improve it then it head on to next mistake we correct it than it becomes next mistake somehow we again correct it than it becomes next. This process goes on until we reach to the end of the path where we are going to meet our success. Thomas Edison while doing invention found 1000 times error which he corrected finally arriving to success in making the invention coming into reality.

Our society has fallen trap of avoid making mistakes and even more difficult to accept the mistakes. If you fail a test than you are a failure or if you make a mistake than you are a culprit. Also Universities and employers evaluate candidates on based on their numbers and grades but we have to understand that our grade does not define our success. I have closely observed that those who achieve "A" grade in school and colleges go as far as landing with some good jobs and getting married performing average in real life but the person having "C" grade all through education emerge as winner in the real life because of very fact accepting mistake he had done. Pickup any example of successful person, you will find most of them are college dropouts like Bill Gates, Henry Ford, Albert Einstein or Mark Zukerberg.

One such person was Thomas Alva Edison who was regarded as "Stupid and junk headed". He attended primary school for a total of three months because of the incident that happened which has changed his life forever. Due to his introvert nature he never talked to any students. His lips were so tightly sewed that he never answered any question even from the threat of punishment. One day he heard the conversation of his teachers talking about him that he was "Mentally retarded" and it wouldn't be worthy to keep him in school. He went home and told his mother about the incidence. His mother anxiously took him to school and made announcement at top of her voice that her son Thomas Alva Edison had more brain than any of the teachers here. His mother never misjudged him and casted him into genius which today also we know as great inventor of all time with having highest number of patents. He made 1094 patent inventions for the benefit of the mankind.

Mistakes let us discover who we truly are and direct us on the path of learning and happiness. Learning from mistakes starts with putting yourself into the situation where mistakes can happen than accepting if mistake is done with confidence and finally courageously making changes but not acknowledge a mistake, ignorance, not to correct and learn from it leads to deeper injury to self.

On the basis of learning experience we can classify the mistake into two. One is careless mistake and other is critical mistakes. Careless mistake are those which carry shallow lessons of learning with them like when you trying to solve mathematics problem and you made some mistake while doing some addition or subtraction or when you spilled a glass of milk on the floor while when you do some critical mistakes it changes the course of your life on the moment notice with real lessons of learning through them. What is the most critical mistake one can do by committing suicide, getting addicted to drugs, pills, failing thrice in ninth grade he was none other than the famous Rap star "Eminem" who learned from his mistakes moved forward and reached the heights of success. Mistakes makes us learn lots of things, we must have courage to accept the mistake. The best way to accept mistake is to be humorous about them for example when one of our friend do some mistake we laugh at him which itself means mistake is acceptable so when we can laugh at mistakes of other why not in our own mistakes? Being humorous about mistakes means we have accepted that we have done mistake and we are ready to learn from it, to bring the change.

Fun Activity to be Practised:-

- Write down your mistakes in piece of paper daily with what you learn from it and stand in front of mirror if you are introvert or in front of family member have courage to speak out. Once you start doing this you will start learning from it with acceptance from your end and others also.

Chapter – Thirteen

"Failure is not fatal"

If you look at the word "Failure" it carries within itself the word "Lure" which means "Tempt to do something especially by offering some form of reward". So when you fail while acting on your dreams or setbacks you are facing along the way of goals set by you, remember one thing that it is just tempting you to put more efforts, to try with more energy, with more creative ideas to enjoy the fruits of happiness, rejoice your victory which it is holding at the end when you succeed in your attempts, this is the reason why failure is always regarded as Stepping stone.

When i was kid my father always told me the story of king Aditya which keeps on reminding me in my failures that it is not final.

Aditya was a brave king. He had won many wars during his reign but things were not same all the time, at early stage when he become ruler he had to fight against a large army four times in number of his soldiers, he was defeated. He had to run for his life.

While running, at night he took shelter in a forest cave. He was very depressed. His courage had left him. He lights a fire in cave and was blankly gazing at the ceiling of the cave. While looking on the ceiling an interesting scene happened.

What he observed a small spider was trying to weave a web across the cave ceiling. As the spider crawled up, a thread of web broke and the spider fell down. Despite of many attempts spider failed to climb, but it didn't stopped and tried to climb again and again. Finally after many attempts spider climbed up and completed the web.

This small incidence of spider gave king Aditya thought "if a small spider can face failure so bravely than I'm a human, why should I give up? I will try with all might until i win." The spider become inspiration and gave strength to the defeated king.

King got out of the cave and gathered his brave soldiers in jungle. He fought against the large army. He was defeated again but now, he would not give up his fight.

King fought again and again against the large army and finally, after many attempts he defeated the large army and regained his kingdom. He had learned a lesson from spider that failure is not final unless you give up.

If you are wise, you will not worry about your failures as j k Rowling said "It is impossible to live without failing at something, unless you live so cautiously that you might as well not have lived at all".

Jk Rowling's share this words of wisdom while commencement of her speech in 2008 Harvard on failure and imagination. Jk Rowling took a steep pathway to success. Fifteen years ago, she was unknown to the world. Rowling's humble beginnings can be traced back seven years after graduating from university, a young divorced mother living in poverty. This is the time when she saw herself as a failure. She had a failed marriage with Portugal TV journalist Jorge arantes, she had no permanent work, and she had a young daughter to take care of.

After her divorce she moved from Portugal to Edinburgh, Scotland near to her sister. These failures caused her so much misery that she suffered clinical depression and she went as far as to contemplate suicide.

She also tried her luck in a career in teaching English as a foreign language. However, in order to get the post, she needed further postgraduate certification although she matriculated herself into this course after her first novel.

The seemingly hopeless situation and her failures became the source of inspiration for her, she began to focus her energies on work that mattered to her most. She wrote the work in different cafes, especially in Nicolson's cafe, which also became a local place of interest. Being a single parent she had to take care of daughter and everyday she can began writing only when her daughter fall asleep. She had to tire Jessica by walking to different cafes and when her daughter sleeps she resume her writing. It proved to be tough and tiresome for Rowling.

She written her first manuscript on her single asset an old type writer in 1995 and entitled it "Harry potter and the philosopher's stone".

When Rowling went for search of publishers her manuscript was turned down by twelve publishing houses. Fortunately, a small publishing house owner Barry Cunningham agreed to publish the book owing to facts that her eight year old daughter loved reading few pages of book and requesting the follow-up texts. This paved her path with huge success, since then Rowling received several grants.

Why do I talk about the benefits of failure? The reason is it transforms us from what we are to what we want to become.

When I read story of Abraham Lincoln, I simply described it with the quote "In this whole world failure loves me a lot and I reciprocate it's feeling by keep on trying". An extraordinary courage and leadership of an ordinary man, whose failures, also can't stop him from being successful.

Abraham Lincoln was born into poverty, Lincoln was faced with defeat throughout his life and it was his courage to continue made him greatest presidents in the United States history.

The incident happened in his office, when he shown the sketch of road to white house. He was listening to the story of a depressed and nervous friend, who was narrating him the failures, misfortune and struggle of his life. As soon as his friend finished his story, Abraham Lincoln told his friend to take glance at the board. When this person minutely glanced at board and read the content, on the board written was the failure list of Lincoln which infused a new ray of hope in person, he got uplifted spiritually and he thanked Abraham Lincoln to showing him new direction towards his dreams.

Let's have look at the path on which he walked leads him to success.

1. 1816 His family was forced out of their home. He had to work on fields to support them which affected his education.
2. 1818 His mother died.
3. 1831 At the age of 21 he was unsuccessful in business.
4. 1832 He ran for state legislature and miserable lost.
5. 1832 in the same year he lost his job; he tried to get into law school but couldn't get in.
6. 1833 Borrowed some money from a friend to begin a business and by the end of the year he was bankrupt. He spent the next 17 years of his life paying off this debt.

7. 1835 was engaged to be married, unfortunately his sweetheart died and his heart was broken.
8. 1836 Gone into depression had a total nervous breakdown and was in bed for six months.
9. 1838 Sought to become speaker of the state legislature but was defeated.
10. 1840 Sought to become elector but again he had to face the defeat.
11. 1843 This time he ran for congress and lost.
12. 1846 Again stood for congress this time he won, went to Washington and did a good job.
13. 1848 Ran for re-election to congress and lost.
14. 1849 He applied for the job of land officer in his home state and was rejected.
15. 1854 This time he ran for senate of the United States and was defeated.
16. 1856 Sought the vice-presidential nomination at his party's national convention and got less than 100 votes.
17. 1858 He again ran for U.S senate and lost again.
18. 1860 Finally elected as president of the United States.

Fun Activity to be practised:-

•   When you fail at something look at the steps where you missed out and reaproach with courage to follow the steps again with a believe you can do it!!!

Chapter – Fourteen

"Never take No for an answer without asking question – Ankit Shende"

Rejection is a myth, it doesn't really exist. Rejection simply means that you have not presented yourself as best as you can, you have not given all that it takes. Most of the people in life go cynical when they hear a no or get rejected and they talked themselves out of it but that is not true. Let me tell you an interesting thing which you have already observed, whenever baby wants something and if you try to say no to him, baby tries with all his might and will not stop until baby gets it. You have to get used to idea that there is going to be a lot rejection and no waiting along the way of your digging the gold out of the mines but the secret of success lies on keep digging and moving forward along the way.

If you face a rejection in whatever endeavour you have taken, you have to remember that you have to keep asking for it until you get a yes. The yes is out there waiting; you just have to hang out there long enough to eventually get yes. One of my friends Nasim is working in sales of life and general insurance; currently he is being promoted to team lead in his company. When I asked him about, how he made up to this position in such a short period of time even when company was downsizing by firing people out of the company at the time of great depression. He simply smiled and told me "I just kept hanging on when people usually quit. People generally quit when they make fifty calls a day and no one shows up to them but i had made up my mind that somewhere there is yes waiting for me and i will not go home unless I hear a yes and close a deal". He continued speaking "At first it was hard for me, as I was not having proper command over language and hardly able to influence people but I kept on calling with a scribbling pad and pen near to me. After every call I started making notes by asking myself where i missed the nodes to close the deal and instead of dropping out like other people, I just doubled the call from fifty to hundred calls that day. Many of the calls ended immediately, some turned into long conversation with people asking tons of questions and after ninety call the next ten people all bought up and from that day onwards I never looked back". Nasim had a ratio of ten percent which is the good ratio for the guy like him, who was not having proper command over language. The point worth noting down is all enrolments came in last ten calls. What if he had given up like other people after first fifty calls and said "This isn't working, it just not worthy efforts as nobody is buying any policy" he would be in the list of the people who got fired.

Rejection word itself carries within the word "ON". It simply sits there asking question to you "Are you still willing to put ON for the next level of testing which will reward you with great success and astonishing results?". The spectacled colonel Harland sanders could be identified as a great example of rejection. He showed people success can be created regardless of your age and your will to keep going on after rejections. Whether you like KFC or not the colonel Haraland Sanders was truly amazing. One of the most amazing aspects of his life was when he reached the age of sixty five, after running a restaurant for several years, Harald sanders found himself penniless. He retired and received his first social security check for one hundred and five dollars but he didn't settled on to it like most of the people do instead he went on for the beginning of life he dreamed off. Colonel sanders was a fellow who love to share his fried chicken recipe. He decided to sell the world his new innovative cool chicken recipe. With meagre resources and great recipe, colonel sanders travelled door to door to houses and restaurants all over his local area. He wanted to partner with someone to help promote his chicken recipe. He started travelling to different restaurants and cooked his fried chicken on the spot for restaurant owners. The legend heard 1009 times "NO" before he heard his first "YES".

He was turned down by one thousand and nine hundred restaurant owners before his chicken recipe was accepted. There he was in front of his first KFC store the deal was that for each piece of chicken the restaurant sold, sanders will receive a small penny of it. By 1964 colonel sanders had 600 franchises selling his trademark chicken. In 1976 the colonel was ranked as the world's second most recognizable celebrity.

There is always some treasure in the trash of rejections. You should make up your mind to never take no for an answer. Others don't know what is possible for you? It is you who determines what is possible for you. Remember that there are 7 billion people on the face of earth, hearing few no doesn't determine you fate. You have to keep moving forward rather than to retreat. My mother is a gynaecologist Dr. Jyotsna mahaskar shende while in the labour room despite of so many rejections by pregnant lady moaning in pain and hearing those words again and again "I can't ". She keeps on motivating and telling the lady to push, the end result is the birth of healthy new born baby without scissor.

There is a funny thing about life while you are driving towards your goal and trying to bring your dream into reality. Life keeps on putting roadblocks on your way several times but when you keep on moving over and over above the roadblock with determination not retreating back; finally it shows the way towards the destiny of abundance to you.

We have to understand that the world in which we live, negativity is spread like a plague and it's the negative surrounding which is pulling us back. Open a newspaper you will find pages fill more with negativity rather than positive and motivating news challenging you to get up from your bed energetically or the television you put on same story repeat here too. Even your immediate surrounding is filled with negative vibes from childhood only if you try do something different you had heard No, anger, criticism for things which are not acceptable and as you grew up you are taught with "Instruction manual of NO in life" what you should not do and develop yourself into adults with possibility blindness.

One such experience happened to me at the time of schooling when I was in the eighth grade, student and teacher were preparing for upcoming event of sub-zonal sports competition to be held at other school. For every event there were selection going on and I was too excited to participate in at least one event but could not able to make it through selection as other boys were stronger than me in competition in every sports whether it was javelin throw or short put throw or 100, 200 meter dash or badminton or long jump. I was eager to participate in at least one of the sports so I looked for event where nobody was going to participate so that I will get a chance to be in school team for sub-zonal meet. After careful peeking in the teacher's selection list I found that nobody was participating in 1600 meter race and I asked "Madam I want to participate in 1600 meter race". To her amuse and laughing she replied to me "Look at you, you are too thin and weak for this race. It require lot of stamina, you can't even going to complete half of the race". Teacher such exclamation towards me infused determination to participate and not to take "No" for an answer. I requested one more time to teacher this time more firmly "I want to participate please write my name in the list". She said "Ok! I will write your name but it's pointless to be stubborn about race when you never ranned even a 400 meter race till now".

Two days after we went to other school where events were taking place and in the afternoon my name called for the event of 1600 meter race. Till noon we didn't bagged any medals on scoreboard so nobody even came forward to cheer me up. I walked calmly towards the track with only aim to complete the race and fortify the words thrown by teacher on to me as I didn't got time to practise. Race started with a shot of airgun and I started running with my head down to see only the track on which I was running. After two laps out of eight competitors two of them fallen down exhausted on the track and I kept running with breathing heavily. As soon as I completed third lap, my schoolmates started cheering up loudly calling my name "C'mon, Ankit you can do it". Sudden spark went on my whole body listening my school mate cheering up and I looked up found there were only four runners left in the race for the last lap. One was running by my side and other two were running only 25 feet ahead. My nose got punctured due to gasping and I was having burning sensation in nostrils but when I saw my teacher standing near to finish line cheering up, it infused forces in my adrenaline to run with full force towards finish line and I just dashed forgetting all the pain to complete the race. Touched the finish line and cracked down on the ground with my head spinning, feet trembling and gasping. My teacher came holding me from shoulder and taken me to stand on winning board. Few moments later when I got my senses back finding that I finished the race in first position.

I still remember the teacher name "Ratna Tondon" and her words after race "This is the lesson we both had learnt today my son and remember this for lifetime, sometimes in life we never know what is possible for us and we walk out of it, hearing a rejection or a "No" but if we try and challenge ourselves enough we could emerge as a winner". The world is ready to say "No" than it is your business to prove them.

We should have positive attitude towards the rejection because if you pick story of any successful people you will find they were rejected many times before they finally succeeded. The other thing we should keep in mind that rejections always leads to bigger and better achievement. You should think, you were rejected because life has some bigger success in stores for you. In 1998 when cofounders of Google Sergey Brin and Larry Page when approached Yahoo for mergers, they had faced in rejection from Yahoo with piece of advice to keep working on their school project and should return when they are grown up but if you look today Google had already taken over Yahoo by purchasing it and eventually is the biggest search engine on the earth with largest market capitalisation company.

Chapter – Fifteen

"Patience use it before you loose it"

We are living in the generation where everything is changing at much pace whether it is technological change or climate and we had developed certain habits as a result of it getting panic to adjust to this pace but one should beware of this destructive pattern. Think of what will happen when you try to drink too hot tea being impatient??? You will get burned, you will not able to feel its taste and aroma but what if you slowly take sip by sip patiently, then you will not only feel it's taste, aroma but it will also give you freshness and happiness. Impatience is a deepest trench to fall while on the way to success. Being impatient is like sabotage; it's an ugly trade which affects not only you but also those around you and fill the life with stress, anxiety, dissatisfaction, fear and anger.

I remember one such incident happened with me when I was a small kid from where I learnt the lessons of patience but started applying recently when faced with crisis producing pattern of sabotage because I too get caught in the pace. One day while wandering in our garden with my father I saw the Oval shaped close shell in the little shed made into home for hens. Pointing out to the little shell with curiosity I asked "Dad, what is this?" My dad smiled and said "Son this is egg, inside shell the process of change is undergoing to become a chicken and as soon as it becomes cute chicken it will be coming out by breaking the egg shell". By giving satisfactory answer my dad went inside for some work but to make peace with my curiosity and excitement I sat there waiting for it to come out.

I waited there almost 2-3 hours for chicken to come out of the egg until my father came back again. My father asked me "Son what are you doing here sitting?". I said "waiting for chicken to come out of egg but nothing really happened till now only to my amazement hen came and sat on it hiding the egg from me".

Once again smile appeared on the face of my father, he said "Son come here, I forgot to tell you that it will take time to happen. You have to be patient". The very next day I got the chance to watch chicken coming out of the egg. Throughout our life we are going to face difficult situations waiting for result but not getting it, at that time we have to give reminder to ourselves that we have to relax and just focus on our work it will going to happen on its time.

The very next thing which is more important to note is generally people get muddled between "Procrastination" and "Patience". When we are able to clearly understand what is the real difference between "Procrastination" and "Patience" than only we will be able to use the tool of patience wisely to shape our success. When we wait for opportunity or some mirage to happen deciding than I will start and end up waiting endlessly is known as procrastination. Patience really means to start taking action, get into the moves with believe to meet opportunity along the way and desired results on its time never early or late is real meaning of patience in terms of success formulae. A pregnant lady cannot become mother on day one itself by giving birth to baby but it takes nine months of patience along with action in terms of care, precaution, healthy diet and other necessary steps to develop foetus into baby with lots of pain while delivering. The pregnant lady knows she will have to keep patience because baby will born on its decided time not too early or too late similarly natures law follow in all field and process it never differentiate so we have to keep patience not getting panic for the result knowing that it will happen on time we have to just keep working towards it, we have to keep pushing towards it, we have to keep putting efforts towards it.

One of my friends Mukesh Malakar understood the concept of patience from the very beginnings; he personally named it "Go with the Flow". He was weak in studies failing twice in school. He always scored lower grades because of his hand writing though he was having quality of keen observation and practically understanding about the machines. Despite of comments, critics given to him "Engineering is not for you", "Don't waste your fathers money", "Go and help your father in his business" but he followed his heart taking admission into the engineering there also he didn't performed well until final year having backlogs in every semester. It was his patience and not to quit attitude which helped him clear the engineering. After engineering also he had to wait for complete one year to get his first job with minimum pay one can get on the other hand many of his batch mates were working with healthy in different Multi National Companies. He kept on working with patience knowing his fruits of hard work will ripe on its time soon he joined the contractual job with "Tata Motors". Later on when contract got over which was for one year he was fired twice out of work but he kept on going with belief in his ability, knowledge and finally just after seven years he is now working as Project Head Consultant in one of the reputed engineering services company with handsome pay, build his duplex home while his batch mates still struggling to reach such heights. During all those time he kept on holding with his belief "Go with the Flow" keeping patience and working diligently towards his goals that destiny will arrive at its own time.

We should think life as a water of flowing river. At the beginning it has very thin stream which with time turns into robust turbulent flow discovering self along the way carrying lots of dirt and garbage thrown, muddled with eroded soil paving through obstacles as rigid as rocks falling from heights of the mountain but having patience to reach its destiny meeting with giant ocean of abundance of success and the desirable things which we want from life. It should be clearly understood that there are no shortcuts to reach the ocean; you have to keep patience while working towards the abundance of success.

The story of Marie and Pierre Curie depicts incredible winning strength of patience over the face of adversity. They had worked four gruelling years of discord, ambiguity and bitter disappointments in search of radium with patience treating tons of residues kilogram by kilogram in their shed laboratory.

There also came time when Pierre belief was weakening with blows of harsh winds for finding the radium. He was ready to give up on his years of research conducting experiment after experiment. He was despair from facing failure in more than fifty experiments but Marie didn't questioned their believe was made of steel. She was determined enough to continue even it takes their whole life in finding radium. She motivated Pierre that we will keep on our research work until we discover the radium even if it takes our whole life.

Finally their hard work and patience came to fruitation one night which she called the "Night of Magic" when magic wand of nature released the secrets of mysterious radium which it was holding on to them. They went to shed together after spending their evening with an ill child after making him sleep. On reaching the shed Marie curiously said to Pierre "Don't light the Lamp" while he was eagerly unlocking the door. When they stepped in together holding each other's arm by opening the door their it was penetrating the darkness with his incredible bluish glow. Their patient labour and sheer determination was rewarded to them in the form of pale and glimmering radium.

Chapter – Sixteen

"This Shall too Pass"

To understand the concept is off much importance because once you understand it, then you can use it for your own good throughout your life rather than memorizing and forgetting it after sometime.

What and why are problems, difficulties or obstacles are in life?

Problems and difficulties we face are just another name of inconvenience in life. It is the situation when you are not comfortable with living and you strongly desire change. They are there to bring new learning experience, growth and change. They come to make you learn how to handle situations and to control the steering of life. You will find no path in your life where there are no obstacles starting from learning to walk, getting degree in college, playing sports or driving a vehicle and luckily if you find one without obstacles it will lead you nowhere. We have mindset to avoid or to run away from problems and difficulties but we should know that we cannot put inconvenience in rug and pretend it is not there. A seed when sowed in soil nurtured around with air and water. It has to go through the pain of heat of summers, face the winds then only it grows into beautiful flower one day. It cannot escape to some other place or wait for situation to settle down then to grow.

Another truth is we human have tendency that we don't care or give value or importance to things which we easily get. It is just like Iron which is available in plenty on earth have less value then gold which is categorised as precious metal. The fact is, if it does not matter to us we should have not care about it or could got upset with it. To have appreciation of what we have and how far we had came or to enjoy success and happiness for any length of time we have to go through challenges.

Long ago there lived a farmer who had herds of cattle. Daily he left cattle's into his field for grazing. One day while grazing an old bull fell into the dry well and grieving out loud enough in pain and panic to be heard by farmer.

Hearing the loud cry farmer went near to well carefully analyzing the situation. He thought sympathized about bull which was too old and wounded if saved then also it will be of no use, it is not worthy to take trouble. Therefore he gathered his neighbours for help by telling them what had happened? He insisted everyone to haul the dirt to bury the old bull in the well and release him from his sufferings.

When bull got realization of situation what was happening? He got depressed and became hysterical but as the crowd continued shovelling dirt an Idea struck in the mind of the bull. He stood straight up waited for load of dirt to arrive on his back and as soon as shovel of dirt landed he would shake it off and step up.

He continues doing this every time laden of dirt falls on his back. "Shake it off and step up" again "Shake it off and step up". Repeating again and again his confidence grown to continue doing the process no matter how painful the blow was. He kept right on "Shaking it off and steeping up".

Finally exhausted bull stepped out of the well triumphantly over the situation of burying him which actually helped him.

Growth does not take place when we give up in panic, bitterness or self pity but it take place when we face them and respond to them. If you have to climb up the ladder of success you have to go through each rung at a time there is no other way round.

Difficulties and problems we face are seasonal they are not going to stay for long and they are definitely going to pass. When difficulties or roadblocks come along the way of your success or dream don't run from it and grip in mind that it is an opportunity for you to excel. We should be like an eagle which comes to know about the storm long before it approaches. Eagle simply fly to some high spot and wait for the winds to arrive.

When the storm hits, eagle stretch and sets its wings in such a way that the wind will pick it up and lift it above the storm leaving the storm raging below. The eagle doesn't escape the storm but it uses the wind that bring the storm as an opportunity to lift it higher and soaring it above the storm.

We have to challenge ourselves when the storms of life come upon us and we can also rise like an eagle above the difficulties that bring sickness, tragedy, failure and disappointment into our lives.

Every problem comes with a definite solution you have to look for it. Albert Einstein once said "The significant problem cannot be solved by the same level of thinking that created them". Sometimes complex problem have simple solutions and sometimes it require creative approach to solve simple problem.

Once in Japan in a soap factory they met with the problem when one of their customers made complain that few soap boxes were empty in the cartoon supplied to them. Observing the problem the factory owner called a meeting with management to tell and Instruct them about the complain to fix it within a week. The management found problem was along the assembly line while machine packing soap in soap boxes misses few of them as it works on timer installed in the machine and to solve this problem they called team of engineers to come up with solutions. After a week different engineers came up with expensive machines ideas to detect the empty soap boxes which will cost company few hundred thousand dollars.

Engineers made machine which was installed along the assembly line and production continued. Within few days factory owner received same complain again from the customer about empty soap boxes. Furious with the issue owner decided to take meeting along the assembly line where packaging of soap is done. All factory workers gathered along with the management people and engineers. Engineers went on to demonstrate the working machine made to solve the problem, while it was unable to produce necessary result of detection of empty soap boxes. They had given few more new solutions for the problem which was again going to cost company with few hundred thousand dollars. An old experienced factory worker was listening carefully became an eye catcher of everybody when he said "I have a solution which will cost company not more than few hundred dollars".

The owner asked the worker "what is your suggestion for the problem?"

The old man replied "If we place a fan near to exit after soap has been filled in the soap boxes, the empty boxes will be thrown away from assembly line due to air from fan" leaving everyone astound with his simple solution to the problem.

Now according to my analysis problems have two subdivisions one is Inherent and other one is Influential. Here Inherent means problem and solution present within us. Most of the time problems is present within and we search outside in surrounding for problem and solutions. Inherent problems can be physical or mental like being handicap, suffering mental disorder or having nervous breakdown or depression or fear and on the other hand Influential means problems or difficulties arouse due to some external factors it can be people like criticizing you while you are working towards your goals or trying to pull you back or putting hindrance along your way to success and environment like earthquake levelling up your factory or fire burning down your shop and house or meeting with an accident and we have to find solution for it.

Vijay Mhaske is an example of Inherent problem born and brought up in Nasik was handicap by birth and for inherent problem solution we don't have to go very far instead we have to search within ourselves. In 2013 when he was in tenth standard he made the software name "Microsoft Surface Sipixels" which can detect the life and age of building, dams, bridges and roads. He was hired by Infosys for his achievement at such a younger age with handsome package. Vijay hands and legs are bent by birth he cannot walk and not even talk properly but once he recognized that problem is within himself instead of getting depressed he focussed on finding solution to thrive more out of life.

Farida Badwai from Ghana is an inspirational example for the people who gets depressed and defeated in front of Inherent problems. After her birth in 1979 she suffered from neurological disorder "Cerebral Palacy" in which body movement and muscles does not coordinate but she not only fought with it instead she started developing her skills and established a company "Logicell". Today more than 130 companies of micro finance worldwide uses her software. She had been awarded as most influential and powerful women in the field of Business and technology. There is no problem in this world which does not come with solution. If you have willingness to fight against the adversity without escaping like most people do you will find solution for it.

In Chinese crisis is written using two characters, one character means opportunity and other means danger it is up to us how we see the problem? Difficulties are inevitable you don't have control over them but how to use it opportunistically is in our hand. When you are facing problem you have to think them as an opportunity to build your character. Influential problems don't have the power of their own to affect you directly; they can only try to influence you, to make you retreat. They should be treated as test to acknowledge what we are capable of doing? What are our strengths? Influential problems present themselves before us so that we should stretch beyond our comfort zone and thrive for more, develop our true character, discover our true potential.

Chad Mureta presented himself as great inspiration to others who are and will be facing difficulties. Chad Mureta was into the business of real estate which gave him sound earnings. His business was running good until the day he met with a car accident which left him bedridden laying on the hospital bed. Adversity began to affect his every part of life he was going out of business because of his physical absence. On the other hand adversity was ready to bring another dish on his plate in the form of mounting medical bills. Soon it was evident to Mureta that he had to find some alternate source of income.

Mureta had routine of reading magazines in hospital. One day while going though magazine came across an article about mobile apps. Mureta was ready to take chance with building apps as he had foresightedness of growth potential with involved risk. He knew every "Business starts with an idea" so he took paper and pencil began working on his idea of app preparing sketches and notes with adequate research about market. Once he was ready with the idea he outsourced all his work to Development Company by taking a loan of 1800$ dollars. As soon as he launched his first finger print pro security app it became sensational in the app store placing his app under best 50 popular app with earnings of 140,000$ for Mureta. Till date Mureta had founded and sold three app companies with 46 apps in the market produced by him. Mureta did not had any technological knowledge but it was his attitude not to had negative effect on him because of all influential problem he faced from meeting with an accident, medical bills, collapsed real estate business, not knowing about technological and programming skills, was bedridden with almost losing his arm.

Once you know that you are having problem or difficulty and its type than comes the most important question in the mind how to tackle the problems or to overcome the difficulties while working towards our goals or dreams? Is there any method which will work every time in every situation or field? In search of such an effective method I had gone through enemurous literatures written and found various solutions for it but the most effective method I found was "Pareto Principle". Pareto Principle explains that our 80% of the problems or difficulties have 20% of the cause behind and if we able to find the 20% root cause we can easily handle the problems or difficulties with ease. For example if a whole class of students making noise when teacher is not there to the level of scrutiny if you figure out, you will find only 20% naughtorious students are the real reason behind it and if you try to focus to control these 20% students you can ultimately control the whole class. It can be applied in every field, situations and circumstances let us suppose if the stock market Indices are falling steeply or rising at much higher rate is mainly due to the movement of 20% large capital companies who have major market capitalisations. Or whether we take an example of Motorbike not getting started what we or else mechanic go for first 20% cause like spark plug or carburettor. Pareto principle is simple yet powerful tool to tackle any problem or to overcome any difficulties.

Chapter – Seventeen

"Once you stop quitting than only you start winning – Ankit Shende"

We all have to face a time when things not go right and we become cynical about life. During those times, when misery keeps beating us harder again and again, we must think of the reason why we have started? Most people quit on themselves, their dreams when they had felt deeper sense of pain while climbing the cliff of success or when they had got burnt their hands while working towards their goal.

Quitting is like electric current which flows through the line of least resistance but a bulb glows only through resistance. One such Iconic person was Charles Schultz, who had faced many challenges but refuse to quit. His uncle had given him pet name "Sparky", after a comic-strip horse named Spark Plug. Sparky had very humble beginnings and schooling seems total failure to him.

He was always on the bottom line of the grades and in eighth grade; he scored F in all the subjects. Slipping on grades was never new to him continuing to high school getting zero in physics, not scoring in Latin, algebra and English. Sport's was also never better match for him although he managed to make it in to the school's golf team, unfortunately he face the defeat there too.

Growing old was not easy for him from the social point of view. No one really cared of him, all through passing his youth, Sparky was awkward socially. He was so intelligently ignored that Sparky was astonished if someone from his classmate ever said hello to him outside of school hours. He was introvert to ask a girl for a date. He had phobia of turning down or perhaps being embarrassed or laughed at. What seems to everyone Sparky was a loser. He accepted his mediocrity and became content with thinking that if things were going to change, they would. Otherwise he would live the life as it comes being a loser.

Apart from this Sparky was having keen interest in drawing. It was drawing which always gives him happiness, he was proud of his artwork. He was so fond of drawing that even no one appreciated it didn't bother him. In fact during senior year of high school, he submitted some cartoons to the yearbook. The editorial board rejected his work. Despite of rejection he continued his hobby. He was so much convinced of his ability that he even decided to become an artist.

As soon as Sparky passed his high school, he tried for Walt Disney studios for work. Studio people asked for samples of his artwork. His artwork doesn't seems worthy to the studio people and was rejected. Despite of his effort, he was again confirmed as a loser.

But Sparky didn't loose his enthusiasm and continued his artwork by creatively telling his own life's story in the form cartoons. Despite of facing so many rejections in life he didn't give up. Instead, he made a character of little boy putting spotlight on his own life as a perpetual looser and chronic underachiever. We all know him very well because it reminded people of their own painful and embarrassing moments of life. This "Lovable loser" character soon became worldwide famous named "Charlie Brown". This loser boy who kept on trying even facing many failure, rejections again and again was none other than world famous cartoonist Charles Schultz. His cartoon strip, "Peanuts," continues to inspire books, printed on T-shirts and Christmas specials, reminding us, as someone once commented that life somehow finds a way for all of us, even the losers.

Sparky's story unlocks the secret principle of life that at the end nobody is loser it's just take some winner longer time. Remember we all are going to face difficulty, discouragement and failures from time to time. It is necessary to hold on to your faith, to handle it with persistent and continue to work on the unique talent god has given us someday we may also become part of successful and iconic inspirational peoples which only comes through hardship.

The strip is the most popular and influential in the history of the comic strip, with 17,897 strips published in all, making it "arguably the longest story ever told by one human being", according to Robert Thompson of Syracuse University. At its peak, Peanuts ran in over 2,600 newspapers, with a readership of 355 million in 75 countries, and was translated into 21 languages.

Certainly lot of people give up on one yard line never trying to discover what they truly deserve or what could be possible for them. One such incident happened with famous artist of 19th century Dante Gabriel Rossetti. An old man approached with few sketches to Rossetti to have suggestion whether they were good or atleast showed some portential talent.

Rossetti looked over them to the level of scrutiny. After going through few of them, he knew the drawings were worthless. Rossetti gently said to elder man "This pictures doesn't seems to have much value and shows very little talent". He continued ahead "I'm sorry for passing such judgement but I cannot lie to you". The man was at scug now yet he approached Rossetti once again apologizing for taking up his valuable time to have a look on few more pictures. Rossetti was kind man so he didn't denie his request and looked over the next few drawings and enthusiastically replied "They reveal exquisite talent, they are good". He further added "Who so ever had drawn posses great potential. He should be provided with necessary help and encouragement becaause from my point of view he has great future".

Rossetti could see old man standing emotionally with eyes filled with tears. Breaking the silence Rossetti asked "Who is this young artisit?", "Your Son".

Old man swallowing the lump with heavy voice said "No...!!! it's me – 40 years ago, only if I had heard your word of praise earlier I would not had became discouraged and given up too soon".

We all have to face or in future have to go through situations where going ahead get tougher and there seems to be no hope to move forward. The more we try to paddle our hands and legs more we get drown deeper inside the trench, where situation takes control leaving us wrecked and we began to quit ready to live mediocre life passing on our experience to other people just to prove our mediocrity to attain self satisfaction but during those times rather than quitting if we have faith it will lead us to tremendous growth and success.

I remember back to 1996 world olympic meet held at Atlanta America. When one woman Keer Strung from the U.S women's olympic team captured the attention of the world with the crowd cheering in the background. The U.S olympic team named "The magnificient seven" went on head to head against their rivals Russians who had dominated the event by pluinging the gold from past 40 years. During her first vault, Kerri badly injured her ankle while landing. Kerri pain was confronting on her face with teammates holding their breathe because they were too close clinch gold and at this moment they cannot throw towel on their dreams.

Coach reached upto her and said "We need you one more time for the gold". Kerri nodded her head went on picking up her all strength and vaulted for second time landing perfectly on her both feet for a split of second and than collapsed on the ground in agony. Kerri performance secured the gold for America.

Later on when Kerri was interviewed about the win she revealed that even though she had injured her ankle during earlier attempt but it became apparent as the competition continued that resposibiiity of bringing gold was on her shoulder "The pain shot feeled like piercing knife" she said "It brought tears to my eyes" but now I have a gold medal. Kerri showned extraodinary courage in the face of agony and the very real risk of serious lifetime injury, where she was still not ready to quit for winning a spot in the olympics.

Chapter – Eighteen

"Forgiveness brings freedom and growth"

Long from centuries we humans are living in the tribes and groups had tendency to be the part of it, do the deeds with the acceptance of the tribe and eventually developed the habit of being resistant to the change as a part of our personality. Therefore whenever someone tries to do something different from the standard measure set by the tribe, people start resisting the change in the form of Ignorance, critics, comments, tantrum throw on the way and trying to pull them back until or unless person pull himself back or the change was acceptable by the tribe. In similar fashion, while working on your goals, dreams there will be time when you will have to face the resistance from the people in the form of critics, comments and tantrum thrown toward you or they will try to pull you back but you have to make up your mind to ignore them, forgive them, also learn from them and continue to work towards your goals, dreams.

The people are more interested in negative this very fact can be observed with journalist, media, and press now days. If you do hundreds of good things you are not in news, nobody takes a note but once you make a mistake you are out there, everybody is interested in it.

On 26 March 2015 India went on to play with Australia semi finals and lost the match, crowd of Indian fans in stadium and also who were watching on television started throwing tantrum, Protesting, criticising talking and posting on social media about the team and expecting Captain M.S.Dhoni should retire from one day international captainship.

Only when Indian team captain M.S Dhoni appeared before the media giving his statement "I think the media should do a nice research take a few days and my advice would be, whatever you decide, write the opposite and that will be facts". Then only people got realization they went on to negative track forgetting all the efforts team had given till semi finals winning straight seven matches.

Rumours travel at much faster rate beyond our imagination and its very in born nature of human when you tell somebody a rumour you add something to it. The person who hears it will give it new colours, little more depth to it making it more attractive and larger in dimension. If you simply ignore it not becoming infuriated, angry they cannot crush or destroy you but once you got influenced with it definitely they will grow, over power you and crush you.

Let us go through fable of bunch of rats participating in a competition. The race was to reach the top of the high tower. Crowd gather around the tower to watch the race and encourage the participants.

The start shot rang out. Honestly none of them believed that rats going to reach to the top of tower because it was too high for little rats. Sooner people started throwing comment "Ah, its too difficult!!! They will never going to accomplish it" or "No there is no chance, the tower is too high".

One after another some of the rats fell off, except those who were adjusting their grip and trying to climb fast higher and higher. The crowd kept on parading on the participants yelling "It's too difficult. Nobody is going to make it!" The more the discouragement ragged the more rats tired and gave up but one of them amazed whole crowd by going higher and higher without giving up.

By the end of the race everybody has given up, except the one who was determined to finish the race and to reach to the top! Finally when he won the race other participants approached the winner and curiously asked "how he managed to reach the top when none of them had been able to do" and the truth was the winner was deaf.

In life also we are going to face negative and pessimistic people, also those who will rain on you to deprive you of your loveliest dreams or they will try to defer you from your goal. You have to become deaf ear when people tell you cannot achieve your dreams because at that time people are strongly focused on your weakness rather than on your strength. They lack the vision as you.

Glugleimo Marconi was taken to psychopathic hospital by none other than his very own friends for investigation and examination by doctors because he made the announcement that he had found a principle through which he can transmit the messages using air as a medium without the help of any physical means of communication like wires. Later on he invented the first machine to transfer the message through air as medium named as telegraph system proving that his dream were not pipe dream. Marconi also developed the system for Radar which is commonly used in air traffic, ships and submarines. In 1909 he shipped one more victory by bagging the Nobel Prize for his work.

We must know information coming our way while working on dreams; goals are like feedback for us. Now let's break the feedback which we get into two major categories one is positive feedbacks which will help you grow, develop your capabilities, expand your horizon and unleash your potentials. On the other hand negative feedback can drown you even more down side of valley if you react to it emotionally.

Here is another thought for you which will dice the criticism, comments by others into your winning numbers. Think what happens when you go to the shoe shiner to shine your shoe. What he do first apply the polish on your dirty shoe, dirt is overtaken by polish still shoe does not shows up but sooner he started brushing over your shoe diligently and finally your shoe comes sparkling. When people are criticizing, commenting throwing all that waste on you, think them as they are putting polish and brushing you and once they are done you will sparkle and outshine among others.

All the feedbacks you are receiving along the way are only form of information. It is you who have decide which information is to be kept or which information is to be left behind. It is just the process, once you start taking action; you will start getting feedback in all form of advice, help suggestions, criticism. You have to use all the information coming your way wisely, revise your plan, readjust your strategy and continue to enhance your knowledge, improve your skills.

Next thing is to learn to forgive them for negative feedback and criticizing you because until and unless you don't forgive them and most importantly yourself, you will be in trap of resentment, hate, anger or revenge which will dissipate all your energy which brings growth. Mahatma Gandhi said "An eye for an eye can make whole world Blind", Buddha said "Holding on to anger is like grasping a hot coal with the intent of throwing it at someone else, you are the one who gets burned" You cannot relieve past until you practise forgiveness and the more prolong you hold on to this negative emotion the more harm they will do. Forgiveness gives you freedom and with freedom comes the happiness; also once you forgive that's where the growth takes place.

Free your soul, body and mind from affliction, emotional vulnerability and resentment or they will use you by practising forgiveness. Many people are making their life difficult unknowingly with their actions, thoughts and imagination by holding on to it.

Chapter – Nineteen

"Sports is the greatest teacher of Life – Ankit Shende"

In true sense sports is the greatest teacher of all time. Although we human never stop learning since from the day we are born till the day we die but from childhood to adult sports teaches us real lesson about how to live our life? How to overcome difficulties? How to be successful? This does not mean we should deny the education through school and college. What we learn in school, colleges, earning a degree is equally important for life to live but how to live a life can be learnt through sports. If you observe closely you will find that life you are living today, you're key qualities, strength, the way you act, your principles, your motivation, most of them had deeper roots of sports knowingly or unknowingly. Let me unravel how sports are greatest teacher of life.

First of all we had practically observed know it that between age one to five the brain has more capacity to develop, to learn and we also believe that if we plant good seeds in the mind of a child at such time he will become gentleman or woman with good moral when child is grown up. But if we look to the level of scrutiny, if we try to question about it or try to find the reason we will find the facts which are working behind the curtains is children learn and grasp fast because at that age mind is like empty glass ready to be filled with whatever information comes to it and another important reason is that everything seems to him like fun, play, sports.

On the other hand when we grew up as an adult we have glass filled with belief, facts and information collected from years. Therefore to learn either we have to replace the old information from the glass or else have to put more effort to get through. We cannot empty our glass completely so what we can do to learn more and fast is to learn with fun, play which make things more interesting.

This fact can be further supported by Einstein theory of relativity concepts when you go to the movie, you will find that two hours passed to quickly and even after weeks later you will remember the story and plot of movie while when you are attending two hours presentation or lectures it feels like too long and after week you will not able to recall even 20% of the information you had been taught. Therefore from this we can box to a conclusion that we learn more when we make things more playful and interesting.

Let's check other aspect why I called sports as greatest teacher of life through some of my life experiences. When I was in tenth grade playing badminton was my hobby. I use to play with one of my friends Varun Tyagi. Varun was extremely talented in terms of sports among our whole school batch mates, so was true with badminton also. He went to play on district events as a part of school badminton team. It was very evident whenever I play with him; I always ended up losing the match. Two years later when I was in 12 standard, In summer holidays I started taking badminton coaching going through rigorous training period of four hours a day. After three months of coaching when one day we both went to play badminton in indoor stadium. We played several matches it was amazing I won all the matches with big difference of points.

The incidence of winning the games and my sports coaching taught me lots of lesson useful for successful living. I learned talent is cheaper than table salts if we practise persistently even a low skilled person can defeat most talented person, my perspective changed about winning which I earlier thought was difficult to beat Varun. The next important lesson I learned was never fall in trap of competition because earlier I always tried to compete with him never tried to improve my skills but later I defeated him because I was concentrated in improving my skill set rather than competing yet there was another pit fall of competition was I lost enthusiasm and interest in badminton once I defeated him as if my goal was accomplished. The competition let your growth stops, we should always work on improving our skills and if we want to compete should be the one we were yesterday. We should always think on how I can improve my life, skills which I was having yesterday. I learned failure is not final until you accept it. I learned how to keep patience while working towards goal, never to quit. I learned if we stretch beyond our comfort zone we will enhance our true potential. I learned there is no difficulty which cannot be overcome.

Few more important lessons which became part of my healthy habits were realised by me today which taught me nothing in life is wasted everything in past you had done was building your future or was going to help you in future. I learned how to focus from playing play station. During those days I played just because of my passion, interest and pleasure it was giving to me but today I know it had helped me a lot. At the time of schooling I love to play and once I grab the remote I would not leave the screen for four to six hour sometime to twelve hours a day. I played with focus of an eagle forgetting about the world during those hours without even blinking eyes. Today this habit helped me in my reading of different literatures.

Therefore it is true all these necessary qualities required for successful living is being develop through sports. I insist you all must play some sports because what you learn through it will help you lifelong for effective and healthy living along with success and being ready to face any adversity.

Chapter – Twenty

"No matter how foolish question appears to be, it will always put you one step ahead – Ankit Shende"

Till now we have checked all the qualities present within you needed to be successful, to fulfil your dream, to accomplish your goal but we all know even if we have all the ingredients of making a dish we still cannot make a dish until we have the knowledge of knowhow, similarly success will be incomplete and we cannot reach our true potential until we don't ask question at every step. It was the spell of questions which led to one of the greatest scientific discovery when a young man lying under the tree relaxing and engaging time in thinking was made awake of the simple event of an apple falling from the tree to the ground. Isaac Newton used the power of asking question to himself looking at the event happened with "Why does the apple fell on the ground?", "Why does it get attracted to the ground?" which eventually rewarded him with the discovery of the important "Law of Gravitation".

Questions are the foundations to excel, learn and expand the horizon of your brain and body, whenever you ask question your brain always comes up with answer to it or look for it, search for it and that's where the growth take place. We all have seen children keep on asking questions continuously not because they want to irritate us but to expand their knowledge, to satisfy there want of curiosity of knowing more, acquiring more, to understand. While reading book if you look closely you will observe I kept continuously asking questions applying same principle and I had jotted few question in my notebook while writing the book how can improve the quality for readers, how can I use my resources to serve more and impart more knowledge so that it can help millions of people to achieve success? Which made me into the process of continuous improvement of the literature.

Questions come from the deep observation when we try to evaluate some things, circumstances and emotions. What we do during process of evaluation we ask questions and try to get answer for it. From studies it is being revealed that the quality of life depends on the quality of question we asked to our conscience because the answer pave to new discoveries about ourselves, new direction to our life. If we don't ask question that's where our growth stops, generally successful people ask better questions that will produce the desire results which they wanted. Similar concept is applicable in every field and prospect of life whether its business, businesses succeed because people evaluate the situation, strategy, market with right question or whether its a relationship, Relationship flourish only when people ask right questions to examine the real reason of conflict or whether it's a sports where sportsman ask better question about the game he is playing, even in politics, politicians win elections by raising the correct question about epidemic, health, water, food, electricity, house, poverty or development.

Questions carry both powering and disempowering energy within itself. Look around you the people depressed or not doing so well instead of their capabilities because they continuously bombard there mind with negative and limited questions "God why me?", "Why this is happening to me?", "Why to try?" or "Why can't I succeed?" and the reasoning faculty of mind will come up with the millions of reason in support to your state of mind to drown you even more down the line but if you interrupt your mind with new right questions like "How can I achieve it?" or "How can I overcome this situation?" you can change the course of your life.

Dr. Roy Plunkett did the same thing by asking the right question. He was a chemist at Du Pont when he made an experiment which failed but instead of getting disappointed with it, he became curious and asked question "Why this happened?" He didn't throw away the test-tube but weighed the tube finding that tube was weighing more than its initial weight. To this astonishment of the result he again asked the question to himself "Why this Happened?" and in search of answer to this questions he unlocked the new important discovery of transparent plastic tetrafluoroethylene commonly known as Teflon now a days.

When you ready to do some work or try to achieve some goals you will have to ask the three vital questions which will improve the quality of work and will sure shot lead you towards the success. Those three questions are related to, First reason behind your work followed by a question why you are working? Second is procedure behind the work means how you are going to do it? And third one related to fruits of your labour followed by what are the results of your work? This three question are really important if you really want success because when you have reason why you are working, you will not quit when difficult times comes and they are going to come by truck load along your way. The next is when you know the procedure means how to do the work you will work effeciently with heading in proper way not blindly. The third one is when you know the outcomes whether positive and negative than you will have contentment. Therefore this three questions are must to design your destiny and accomplish your dreams.

Fun Activity to be practised:-

- Follow the art ask of asking question in every activity by attaching three words to them, they are Why, How, What!!!

Last Chapter

"Love is the master key that opens the gates of happiness – Olive Wendell Homes"

Before starting this last chapter, I have single question to ask you before giving you final and most precious gift of life. The question is why you want to achieve something, fulfil some goals or dreams, and acquire money, fame or success or to do some social contribution???

Why???

Stop and think about this question for a moment and I guarantee you that majority will come with only one answer in mind and heart that is "Happiness". If you are thinking that I want this thing or achieve this dream because it gives me satisfaction or peace or to show people what I'm or fame or money or success all reasons you think are not vague but only different meaning to your single goal of life that is "Happiness". Ultimately doing that thing or achieving that goal or acting on your dream or acquiring that huge some of wealth or success or fame or some sort of satisfaction or peace of mind leads you to joy and happiness.

Let's begin this last chapter of the book which is about Love. Love is the only driving force which can move mountains. Whatever your purpose may be to accomplish whether some major goals you like to achieve, some social contribution you want to do or you want to change something, some dreams you want to fulfil or some fame and success you are looking for. For that you have to do one thing fall in love with your dreams, work, goals you want to achieve. As you pour your heart out there in the things you want to do, dreams you want to make reality, work or goals you want to achieve, whatever it may be. What You will observe that as you pour your heart out there and started loving things, your work, your dreams the miracle starts happening and things along your way will become easy and I assure you that the day you emerge as winner in life will not be too far then.

There is an old fable which we all have heard many times in our life but never practically used in our life, so here goes the story. There was a family living in small house at the end of beautiful and elegant town. They were very kind and generous people. One day husband went to work as usual and woman came out after finishing her course of cooking for family to have some fresh air in her garden. When she came out she saw three old men having long white beard dressed in white robs were sitting in front of house gate. Looking strangers sitting on the gates, she walked up to them and said "I don't think, I know you but looking at you all I find you must be hungry. Please come in and have something to eat". They asked in unison "Is the man of the house at home". She replied to their concern "No, he is out". "Then we cannot come in, we will wait here" they said. In the evening when her husband came back from work she told him about the incidence. He after listening instructed "Go tell them I am home and invite them". The woman went and invited all three of them as her husband told.

But the old men denied the invitation saying "We do not go into house all together".

"Why is that?" surprised by their answer lady asked furiously.

119

One of the old men came forward and started explaining by pointing his finger towards one of his friends "His name is wealth, the other one is success and my name is love". Continuing he said "Now go in and discuss with your husband which one of us you want in your home".

The woman went inside to convey her husband what they said. Hearing this husband over joyously said "Well in that case, it would be nice to invite wealth let him in and fill our home with wealth". Wife disagreed with thought said "My Dear, why don't we invite success". Their daughter in law was listening to their conversation from the corner of a room. She interrupted them while jumping in middle of their conversation with her own suggestion "I think it would be wise and much better if we invite love, our home will be filled with love!".

Agreeing to her husband said to her wife "Let us heed with our daughter in law's sound advice, go and invite love to our home".

The woman agreed and went out to invite love she said "Love please come in and be our guest for tonight" with smile love stood up and started walking towards the house. After few moments the other two old men also got up and followed him. Again leaving lady surprised by the act, she asked "I only invited love, why both of you coming in?"

The old men replied together "Well if you would have invited either one of us both wealth and success. The other two would have stayed out but since you invited love we have no choice because wherever he goes, we follow him. Where there is love, there is also wealth and success". We wish for you Where there is pain, we wish you peace and mercy. Where there is self-doubting, we wish you a renewed confidence in Your Ability to work through them. Where there is tiredness, or exhaustion, we wish you understanding, patience, and renewed strength. Where there is fear, we wish you love, and courage.

The moral of the story have clear message that with love everything is possible, whether you want to achieve goals, dreams, want to do some major contribution, success, fame, money etc. You just have to do one thing that is to fall in love, with yourself, with what you do, your character, your work, the action you take towards your dreams, goals. The essence of love is only enough to fulfil all your desires, attract the things and put the joy, excitement and happiness in your life.

While you read this chapter you will come to know my single purpose of writing this book is to get pass your mind, to not only motivate you but also to make you slow down your pace of running towards mere materialistic things and to look into yourself and your life, to look into the life of people around you and your loved ones and to enjoy, share and fill every moment of this journey of life with happiness While going towards your destiny sometimes in life we forget the real purpose of our life "To be Happy". While running towards your goals, acting on your dreams we get so involved that at the end we find that we didn't lived at all. As you achieve the things you want, the dream you turn into reality, the money and fame that you acquired with your hard work, determination and passion you will find that it was your journey towards your destiny that brings you more happiness, that gets lock in your memory, that brings smile on your face while standing on the board of victory.

My destiny, goal and dream of life is to "Love and to be Loved" because I personally believe that "Love is your destiny, everything else is detour on the road of life, that takes you away from your goal of happiness." My dream is to use my gifts and talent to help under privileged, depressed and suppressed

121

peoples to build the life they dreamed off. My mission can be summoned up with great Japanese lines "give a man a fish you feed him for a day. Teach a man to fish and you feed him for lifetime."

I came across one such personality whom I considered truly great iconic person was late Dr. Richard Teo. Dr. Richard Teo was most inspiring person who truly understood the meaning of true happiness, love, sharing and the real purpose of life. Therefore when he truly discovered the true joy, love and sharing, he came forward with his vast abundance of wisdom and knowledge to convey his message to awaken the spirits of people during the critical years of his life when he was on the journey to his deathbed. He was born in year 1972 in an average poor family but he was inborn gifted with talents which he nurtured from early ages of his life being good in academic, sports and leadership along with his highly competative nature. He began his early years of life with typical mindset of today's society that to be happy you should be successful and to be successful you should be rich. This thought had been so much preluded in the people's heart that they considered you successful if you are rich and famous so it was true for Richard also who was hungry searching for the way to be one of them. He graduated as doctor amongs the brightest students by winning scholarship for pursuing speciality in opthalmology and having two patents registered on his name one for medical device and another for use of the lasers for treatment of eyes. At first Richard was a trainee in opthalmology but his strong desire to earn money could not keep him their for longer. He became impatient looking at his some of friends earning ransome of money doing private practise. Therefore he looked into the opportunity of making money in the field of asthetic medicine, he quitted his internship in opthalmology and went for making career in asthetic medicine. During those days people were not willing to pay much for healing. People use to become argumentive to pay even 30$ dollars in consultation.

He was still far behind his dreams of becoming rags to riches till the day he recognized the potential of being an beautician that same people who were not ready to pay for medication much are willing to pay thousands of dollars for liposuction, breast augmentation. He was not ready to let this opportunity slip by his hand so he jumped into becoming medically trained beautician started doing all kinds of procedure required from liposuction to breast augmentation to eye lid surgeries and many more. Within short span of time he became one who was talk of the town with his clinic waiting time raising from one week to jumping across the mark of three months in the calendar. His work was overloaded to such a extent that he had to employee doctors making him famous cosmetic surgeon in singapore but this all didn't satisfied his money building hunger instead he became so obsessed that he wanted more and more of it. He went on for opening of another clinic in the Indonesia to attract more patients and bring home more business.

With all his truck load of money he went on for shop all luxuorious stuff, he once dreamed off starting from buying convertable ferrari to building of the gold class bunglow of 30-35 $ million dollars which were equivalent to buying home at baverly hills. In his spare time he went on for car club gatherings to car racing and to mix around with rich and famous people's. Richard was also too cautious for health pushing himself hard daily in the gym. He was at pinnacle of his life achieving everything thinking that he had full control over everything in his life running endless rat race becoming today's successful society product.

His life transformation began on the day when he was diagnosed with the stage – 4 teriminal lung cancer. He went through all the test in shock of diagonsis from MRI to PET scans for confirmation of cancer because moments ago he was having everything with full control over his life and very next moment he was hammered out. The CT scan of lungs had clearly showned he was having tens of thousands of milliaries tumour. The sudden blow came crushing on to his life, he went into severe depression but during those down moments he came to realization of what true happiness means. It was not in all of his trophies that he won, not in car and house he owned that didn't bring happiness to him because he cannot hug his ferrari to sleep and feel comfortable with his posessions during his time of anxiety and pain but the real joy came from sharing, loving and interacting with people around him who understood his pain and his happiness, who genuinely cared for him. Coming to this new mental awareness he didn't stop there only instead he went on to share his wisdom with others, to give helping hands and words of encouragement to others.

He had done remarkable work for others during the months closure to his meeting with death uplifting others and left on his words of wisdom in the form of speeches available and distributed all over so that millions of people can be benefitted from it. You can also have copy of his speeches by sending request to his family and friends.

He made focused on his past mistake depicting in true sense your very own reflection about persuasion of the wealth which only brings momentary satisfaction not true joy, so that people should understand the real purpose and joy of life comes only from loving, sharing and helping. Once you are on your deathbed you cannot expect your car or house to comfort you No absolutely not, holding and thinking about them will bring zero percent satisfaction. The truth is when you know you are going to die soon your whole perception changes you will start doing things differently. You will focus only on things which are essential for you. Yet another crucial quality what Dr. Richard taught was that true happiness doesnot comes from serving yourself but it actually comes from serving others. He was being Doctor was trained to be compassionate which he didn't learned in those early days while he was on House Job in oncology department. He witnessed all kinds of patients sufferings, pains and struggling over last few breathes but it wasn't realy to him just a part of job which he learned later through hardships but while going through sufferings he not only encouraged other cancer patients but also consulted them, taking care of them, providing services to them.

We all are in the trap of this rat race but sooner or later we have to realize this fact either going through hardships or learning lessons that greater joy will only follow us when we are pursuing real purpose of life with love, sharing and helping. When we head towards this direction of life definately joy will fill our life with different colours of true happiness.

"Practise the Law of Increasing Return"

At last I would like every one of you to practise "The law of Increasing return" also called the Nature's law of abundance which is applicable throughout the universe on every living thing. Nature gives us everything without expectation and loses nothing while other way round we humans either give with some expectation or not ready to give and thus loses everything we should learn to give without expectation it will bring true happiness, peace and self contentment. Now the question comes why I called this law of increasing return? Because I practically observed it, experimented with it and deduced results out of it. When you give something thinking that you had abundance of it, to share without expectation what you will observe after sometime your reserve of same resources which had been given is automatically increased from other channels. In ancient times people used this technique as a part of their living called teething which means giving tenth part of what you had earn as a charity or someone who is in need.

Well this is interesting to note that everyone of us is following this law unknowingly in some part of our life yet if we observe it and able to apply it in every area of our life, we will not only have abundance but we will also fill our life with happiness and joy. Poor people practise this law in the form of love. They think, they had abundance of love and scarcity of other resources so they believe in giving love to others and in return they get abundance of love. Therefore if they are able to acknowledge that they had abundance of everything and ready for teething without expectation soon they will find that abundance is following their footstep back home. There clog thinking of lacking other resources or basic amenities so they cannot teeth is stopping nature to provide them with it. Similarly rich people think they had abundance of money and give to other without expectation and in return nature gives them back more riches from other sources. It is of haste to think either government or external factor or luck is making rich people rich and poor poorer because root cause lies in each of us, it is we who are responsible for our state.

One of my friends Varun Tyagi followed law of increasing return but hardly even noticed it. He has habit of helping others without expectation. You can call him in any part of the day round the clock for help; he will be there to help you out. According to law of increasing return when you once think that you had enough of something and ready to provide service without expectation than abundance follow you. Therefore nature was always flowing abundance of the resource from other channel because he was always in cord with the law of increasing return. People were and are always ready to help him out in his day to day life, always available to provide him and his family services required.

The most influential iconic person whom I found to be in cord with this Nature's law of increasing return is Manoj Bhargava. Currently he is in the Forbes list of Billionaires who made from rags to riches. Manoj was born in Lucknow in 1963. He was with family relocated to America in 1967 when his father decided to pursue P.H.D at Wharton. Bhargava started testing his hands in business from very early age. He was always good with numbers therefore he joined Princeton college for studies but soon he found college studies in cumbersome therefore he left the college in middle to follow his own way of learning which will be helpful in successful living. In 1974 he moved to India and spent almost 12 years in monasteries to learn how to still his mind and continue his education of practical living.

Manoj returned to the U.S on request of his family to support his father in their plastic business. Soon there business started showing steep rise as Manoj joined in with his innovative ideas, marketing strategies and hard work. They became one of the major players in the PVC business. Finally he sold his Indiana PVC business to a private equity player. Later on he started new venture of manufacturing energy drinks named 5-hours energy by getting inspired in trade fair by one such product and coming up with his new innovative product apart from others.

During all this year Manoj Bhargava practised the teething giving major part of his income in charity. Although Bharagava never wanted fame he always worked and done charity in silence but government was hindering his path to do good for others therefore he has to made his appearance before public and chasing media. Bhargava had given away one billion dollars in charity along with setting of non profit organisation Hans Foundation which has funded more than four hundred charity project like Kamala Nehru Memorial Hospital for cancer treatment for the poor people. Today his company has crossed the mark of one billion dollars in sales year wise. He also announced later to give away his ninety percent of earnings to charity while today his product controls ninety percent of the U.S energy market. Manoj Bhargava has literally produced before us the practical example of law of increasing return. He walked in accordance with the nature's law of giving and abundance followed him. He closely observed and infused in his life how the nature always giving without expectation and henceforth abundance followed.

Author Bio

I had done Engineering in Industrial and production in year 2007 from government engineering college Bhopal after that I went to try my hands on business of tours and travel with one of my friends Ashish Ingle and collaboration with some agents in this business getting successful in the business in short period of six month we moved on for explore new experience in the field of stock market opening a wealth management firm with name Big Paisa which unfortunately run into losses during the market crash of November 2008 although we had achieved far better results and experience along this journey including few of my articles about market research getting published in Informed Investor one of the weekly magazine circulated all over India. Along with opening of Big Paisa we had also worked with Bonanza stock broking firm as an employee. Later I had done Post graduate Diploma in Advance computing from ACTS- CDAC Pune in feb 2010. I had also done M-Tech (Master's in Technology) from COEP (College of Engineering Pune) by clearing GATE examination from year 2011-13. During all those year I had changed 24 Jobs currently summing up my all experience to use for the welfare and upliftment of younger generation, underachievers to achieve success in any endeavour they take and this book is first small step towards it. Apart from this I like Exploring new places and culture, meeting people and off course adventure.

Printed in the United States
By Bookmasters